What Does
the Bible
Say About... **?**

Friendship

"What Does the Bible Say About...?" Series
Ronald D. Witherup, P.S.S.
Series Editor

What Does
the Bible
Say About... **?**

Friendship

Laurie Brink, O.P.

New City Press
Hyde Park, New York

Published by New City Press
202 Comforter Blvd.,
Hyde Park, NY 12538
www.newcitypress.com

Cover design and layout by Miguel Tejerina

Biblical citations are taken from the New Revised Standard Version
©1989 Division of Christian Education of the National Council of
the Churches of Christ in the United States of America.

Library of Congress Cataloging-in-Publication Data

What does the Bible say about Friendship
Library of Congress Control Number: 2019939385

ISBN 978-1-56548-693-5 (paperback)
ISBN 978-1-56548-694-2 (e-book)
ISBN 978-1-56548-697-3 (series ISBN)

Printed in the United States of America

Faithful friends are a sturdy shelter:
whoever finds one has found a treasure (Sirach 6:14).

To Betsy Pawlicki, O.P.,
Marge and Dennis Colgan,
and Cathy Howard, O.P. (R.I.P.)

Contents

Series Preface

The Bible remains the world's number one best-seller of all time. Millions of copies in more than two thousand languages and dialects are sold every year, yet how many are opened and read on a regular basis? Despite the impression the Bible's popularity might give, its riches are not easy to mine. Its message is not self-evident and is sometimes hard to relate to our daily lives.

This series addresses the need for a reliable guide to reading the Bible profitably. Each volume is designed to unlock the Bible's mysteries for the interested reader who asks, "What does the Bible say about...?" Each book addresses a timely theme in contemporary culture, based upon questions people are asking today, and explaining how the Bible can speak to these questions as reflected in both Old and New Testaments.

Ideal for individual or group study, each volume consists of short, concise chapters on a biblical theme in non-technical language, and in a style accessible to all. The expert authors have been chosen for their knowledge of the Bible. While taking into account current scholarship, they know how to explain the Bible's teaching in simple language. They are also able to relate the biblical message to the challenges of today's Church and society while avoiding a simplistic use of the biblical text for trying to "prove" a point or defend a position, which is called "prooftexting"—an improper use of the Bible. The focus in these books is on a religious perspective, explaining what the Bible says, or does not say, about each theme. Short discussion questions invite sharing and reflection.

So, take up your Bible with confidence, and with your guide explore "what the Bible says about friendship."

Introduction

"And then there was the time your father saved that guy's life," Cy recounted. "He went right into a burning building, smoke pouring out everywhere, and dragged the guy out." My family and close friends had gathered at the local barbeque restaurant after my father's funeral to remember him and console each other. The memories poured out like an oral biography of a man I only knew as "Dad." His Knights of Columbus friends remembered my father, a very large man, standing in the middle of the intersection blocking traffic to collect money for the local charity. His bright yellow apron read "Help the Handicapped," a situation one motorist suggested that he would find himself in if he didn't move out of the way! As Dave, one of his workers, retold, one morning my father surprised his employees by taking them to a Cincinnati Reds baseball game . . . a five-hour drive away! It was the first time Dave had been outside the county of his birth. At that meal after the funeral, my family and friends feasted on corn bread and shredded pork, and on the memories of a life made full through love and friendships.

If I know anything about making and maintaining friendships, I learned it from my folks, who valued friendship as one of God's greatest blessings. They were not alone in that assessment. Across time, cultures, religions, and races, friendship has been highly valued. In the Book of Genesis, Abraham is instructed by God to leave his homeland and travel on a promise. His immediate fidelity is credited to him as righteousness. But throughout God and Abraham's relationship, the latter is not just a docile supplicant. Abraham questions, seeks clarification, and even debates with God (Genesis 18:16-32). The relationship depicted between God and Abraham will lead the author of the Book of Chronicles to describe Abraham as God's beloved friend (2 Chronicles 20:7). Numerous other biblical examples will be explored in chapter 1.

The ancient Chinese philosopher Confucius (551-479 BC) and the Greek philosopher whose writings form the backdrop of much later Christian theology, Aristotle (384-322 BC), proposed that friends bring one another joy and are necessary for the good order of the state. According to Confucius, "Is it not delightful to have friends coming from distant quarters?"[1] Writing a century later in the West, Aristotle would echo him: "For no one would choose to live without friends but possessing all other good things."[2]

The Santi Parva, or Book of Peace, from the Indian epic poem, *The Mahabharata*, offers the ruler advice on choosing the right friends. "I am of the opinion that neither swelling wealth, nor relatives, nor kinsmen, occupy that place which well-wishing friends occupy. A friend capable of listening to beneficial counsels, and also of doing good, is exceedingly rare."[3] Islam, too, promotes and encourages friendships that lead one to greater fidelity to Allah:

And the believers, the men and the women are friends one of the other; they bid to honor, and forbid dishonor; they perform the prayer, and pay the alms, and they obey God and his Messenger.[4]

Reading Friendship Inclusively

Various historical periods and cultures may have defined friendship differently, but they nonetheless acknowledge the place that friendship has in society. But most of our ancient literature is the product of male authors writing in patriarchal societies. As the editors of *The Oxford Book of Friendship* note, "In the past women have written less about friendship because they have written less about anything; or less of it has survived."[5] Though the statement might be read as if women have spurned the pen for other pursuits, the historical reality is that women often had less opportunity to produce literature, philosophical treatises, or historical monographs. This reality, coupled with a seeming bias against women's friendships, led Vera Brittain to write,

From the days of Homer the friendships of men have enjoyed glory and acclamation, but the friendships of women, in spite of Ruth and Naomi, have usually been not merely unsung, but mocked, belittled and falsely interpreted.[6]

The author of First Timothy seems to uphold a negative view of women's friendships when he admonishes that young widows be remarried rather than rely on the church for support, since, left without household responsibilities, "they learn to be idle, gadding about from house to house; and they are not merely idle, but also gossips and busybodies, saying what they should not say" (5:13). Women's perspectives on friendship have only recently been considered, so as "one looks back across the landscape of interests in this [topic of friendship], as with so many other matters, the tone is almost wholly and relentlessly masculine."[7] The sixteenth-century author Michel de Montaigne bears this out when he writes that "the normal capacity of women is, in fact, unequal to the demands of that communion and intercourse on which the sacred bond [of friendship] is fed; their souls do not seem firm enough to bear the strain of so hard and lasting a tie. . . . There has never yet been an example of woman's attaining to this, and the ancient schools are one in their belief that it is denied to the female sex."[8]

A society that saw a woman as a misbegotten male (Aristotle, and repeated by noted worthies such as St. Thomas Aquinas) or blamed her for original sin (St. Augustine) wore a particular set of patriarchal lenses. In order to read, appreciate, and draw meaning from these ancient texts for our topic on friendship, we are obliged to add a new lens to our spectacles: what feminist scholars call a hermeneutical or interpretational lens of suspicion. In essence that means we critique what we read before we adopt its tenets wholesale. We cast a cautious eye toward Aristotle, we filter Aquinas, and we must even be a bit suspicious of the biblical text. Remember, while we hold the Bible to be the Word of God, these are historical documents written with "full instrumentality" at a particular moment in history within a particularly patriarchal society.

So while the ancient literature most often describes male friendships, with the aid of a hermeneutical lens of suspicion we can retrieve those ideas that have relevance for men *and* women today. The Athenian society of Aristotle and the medieval world of Aquinas are long since gone, but we can still recognize the importance of friendships both in forming and sustaining societies and in promoting and enriching faith. Though the twenty-first century is decidedly a different world, we would agree with the philosophers that friends form a bridge that allows us to cross from the safety of family into the complexity of society.

An Outside Insider

My mother tells a story that I doubt my brother remembers. When my father was stationed in Morocco, we lived on a military base in the enlisted housing section. Every evening my mother and the neighbor would meet in the middle of the street. This ritual had nothing to do with their duties as Navy wives or even their own friendship. Rather, they would have to separate their sons, who wailed pitifully that their play had ended for another day. "Bye Charlie," my four-year-old brother would cry. "Bye Bradley," his little friend would return. "Bye Charlie," "Bye Bradley," until each was finally corralled into his respective duplex.

As children, our playmates are the first outsiders to break open the primary unit of our family. Whereas our relatives may become our friends, their primary relationship to us is defined by their role with respect to us within the family. Our mother, our father, our sibling, our grandparents, etc. They hold a pride of place in nature and nurture, and without whom we have neither history nor legacy. But as Jem wisely noted in Harper Lee's *To Kill a Mockingbird*,

> You can choose your friends but you sho' can't choose your family, an' they're still kin to you no matter whether you acknowledge 'em or not, and it makes you look right silly when you don't.[9]

Our friends we choose; our family we don't. As children, our friends are our first elected relationship outside the bounds of family. The further we move beyond the confines of our home, the more opportunity we have for finding and making friends. Correspondingly, the greater our maturity, the better the capacity we have for maintaining those relationships. The first-century BC Roman senator and orator Cicero recognized that only with age and wisdom are we able to enter into lasting friendships. "This, given the experience it brings, allows one to give careful thought to the quality of possible friends, for one must aim to respect and revere as well as love them, and they must therefore be worthy of both."[10] My junior high school criteria for a friend was whether she liked the same television shows that I did, and did not like the same boy that I did. I hope I have become a bit more discerning as I have aged.

Where Are We Going?

In my research, I've noticed that the Bible has a lot to say about "friends," but those "friends" might not look as we expect. In order to more fully explore friendship in the Bible, we will follow a person-centered path. We will begin with our questions and concerns about our own friendships and look to Scripture for guidance. In the first chapter, "Friends with Benefits: Redefining Friendship," we explore how to recognize a true friend and what the Bible says about friendship.

In chapter 2, we will ponder a question I hear frequently from my own peers: "Can I be friends with my kids?" Turning to the Bible, we will look to Jesus and his own encounters with his family. How are we to understand what Jesus says about our familial obligations, and how do we translate that into our own day and time?

Chapter 3 addresses the question: "Is my spouse also my friend?" Song of Songs describes the euphoric search for the beloved, but what happens after the honeymoon? What stories and encounters in Scripture shed light on befriending or renewing one's friendship with a spouse or partner? On this topic, Abraham and Sarah have much to share (Genesis chapters 12–23).

Sirach clearly understood that sometimes good friends fail us (Sirach 22:20–22). Chapter 4, "When Good Friends Make Bad Mistakes: Recovery and Reconciliation," acknowledges the reality of broken friendships and the hope of repairing them. Barnabas comes to the aid of Saul after his dramatic encounter on the road to Damascus (Acts chapter 9), and the two launch an evangelizing mission to the Gentiles (Acts chapters 13–14). But after all they had gone through together, a disagreement about personnel severs their relationship (Acts 15:39–40). The stories of Peter's denial and Judas' betrayal are intertwined with Jesus' washing the disciples' feet (John chapter 13). How does Jesus respond to the profound disappointment of his disciples who fall away? John chapter 21 presents a heart-rending scene of reconciliation that demonstrates all is never lost.

And while we hope for reconciliation with our dearest friends, sometimes the reconciliation that needs to happen is within us. Chapter 5 touches home as we look to the topic of "Befriending Myself: Moving beyond Personal Limitations." For too many of us, our experiences of self-loathing or encounters with violence or profound personal disappointments leave us estranged from our very selves. The stories of Moses (Exodus chapter 2), Hannah (1 Samuel chapters 1–2), and Paul (2 Corinthians chapters 4–5) are poignant reminders that personal suffering and tragedy need not be the defining moment of our stories. Befriending ourselves puts us on the path to becoming friends of God, the topic of our final chapter.

"What a friend we have in Jesus," so the familiar church song echoes. And indeed, Jesus calls his own disciples "friends" (John 15:15). In chapter 6, "What a Friend We Have in Jesus: Becoming Friends of God," we culminate our investigation of the Bible on friendship by exploring the topic of friendship with God. Our family, children, spouses, companions, and imperfect pals all teach us how to make, maintain, and grow friendships, leading us to our ultimate goal: becoming friends of God. We will explore Abraham's long friendship with God, and Moses' roller coaster relationship with the God who leads him. We will ponder how chance encounters with strangers can bring divine insights that we only recognize after the fact. We'll join the disciples at the Last Supper and hear Jesus acknowledge that they are no longer servants; they are now his friends. We will see how one's life can be utterly redirected, renewed, and grace-filled by taking God's hand in friendship. And we'll learn that same opportunity awaits us.

For Reflection:

Make a friendship timeline. Mark your birth and conclude with today. Along the line, jot down the names of your friends. Who was your first friend? What do you remember about him or her? Who was your best friend? Have you had several best friends during your life? Would you include your family members as friends? Name those people who are casual friends and those who are intimate friends.

As you mark their names along your life timeline, take a moment to remember them and the significant experiences with them that come to mind. Thank God for the friends in your life.

Chapter One

Friends with Benefits: Redefining Friendship

Introduction

A young woman compares her parents' Facebook page with her own, laughing that they only have a handful of "friends," while she has thousands. The commercial then cuts to her parents and their friends enjoying a beautiful drive on the open road. Back to the young woman who sits alone before her computer screen and laughs at a video, "That can't be a puppy!" The commercial played off the developing redefinition of the term "friend." In the digital age, "friends" are those whom you grant access to your page, so that they can "like" or occasionally comment on something you have posted. To help you build your "friends," Facebook will even suggest the names of other users who may share a marginal connection with you or your other "friends." Or you can purchase "friends" to boost the numbers on your social media account.

The cheapening of the quality of friendship reached an all-time low for me when my niece explained a practice popular among some young adults. "Friends with benefits" means you may occasionally use your friends to satisfy your sexual desires with no strings attached. It would seem that the use and misuse of friendship language is endemic in our social-media-driven society. To allow the continued dilution of the term, and I'd say, downright corruption of it, is to lose sight of one of humanity's greatest gifts, that of friendship. When we call someone our friend, what do we mean? That answer used to be less complicated before the advent of social media. Now we measure our friends in the number of "likes" we get, and we "unfriend" someone virtually if we no longer want to see a posting of yet another cute cat video. *The Oxford English Dictionary* has even included this virtual friendship among its definitions of "friend."[11] Throughout this book, we will mostly be focusing on the more traditional definition of friend as persons with whom one has developed close and informal relationships of mutual trust and intimacy.

Will You Be My Friend?

How we define friendship and how we behave with others have significant implications for our larger society. In fact, ancient philosophers like Aristotle believed that democracy itself was built upon the maintenance of friendship. And since his understanding of friendship forms the foundation of today's definition, we will summarize the ideas of Aristotle on the topic and introduce how Thomas Aquinas reinterpreted those ideas for a Christian context.

Aristotle held that friendship is essential to living a good and useful life, and he recognized three different types of friendship. The first is utilitarian. We become _Kristine_ friends with others because the relationship is mutually beneficial. The second type of friendship is centered on _Mo_ pleasure and enjoyment. The third type of friendship is the truest kind since it is predicated on virtue and love. _Johnnie_ Of the three types of friendships, the utilitarian and the pleasurable are fleeting since they are based on transitory things. Once the need is met and the pleasure fades, the reason for the friendship evaporates. When we ponder past friendships that have faded, we may discern that they were based on either usefulness or pleasure. Aristotle describes the fleeting friendships of youth as examples. But while the friendship may be transitory it is no less a friendship, offering to the friends a mutual benefit and opportunity for personal growth. We may no longer stay up all night chatting with our girlfriends about the trials and tribulations of our teen lives, but those nocturnal conversations were formative to our growth as social beings. The locker room antics showed us how to interact with others, value team effort, and suffer through loss and celebrate victory.

The third category, virtuous friendship, is highly prized. Aristotle saw such a friend as another self, so that what people would desire for themselves, they also desired for their friends. Ancient historian Diogenes of Laertius reported that to the query, "What is a friend?" Aristotle replied, "A single soul dwelling in two bodies."[12] To the Roman orator Cicero (106–43 BC), this friend was also a second self.

What is sweeter than to have someone with whom you may dare discuss anything as if you were communing with yourself? How could your enjoyment in times of prosperity be so great if you did not have someone whose joy in them would be equal to your own?[13]

This last sentiment is echoed in the Book of Ecclesiastes (also called Qoheleth, "the Preacher"):

Two are better than one, because they have a good reward for their toil. For if they fall, one will lift up the other; but woe to one who is alone and falls and does not have another to help. (Ecclesiastes 4:9-10)

These are the friends who have become such a part of the fabric of our life that when they come to Thanksgiving, our children call them "aunt" or "uncle," though there is no blood tie.

Aristotle recognizes virtue or character friendship as the highest form of friendship, since it leads to the human being's highest potential, what we would call happiness. St. Thomas Aquinas reinterprets this through the lens of love, so that charity friendship is the activity that culminates in happiness, and "describes a person who has reached the highest possible development proper to a human being."[14] According to Aristotle, such a friendship demonstrates beneficence, mutuality, and betterment. Building on Aristotle's definition, Aquinas explained these aspects in light of our desire to be friends with God and of the importance of charity. But beneficence or doing good for another does not alone mark one as a friend. In fact, we need only remember Jesus' charge to do good to those who hate us (Luke 6:27) to realize that good works do not establish a friendship. For a relationship to develop, there must be reciprocity. We have all experienced relationships that we thought were friendships but discovered that mutuality was missing. Our loving actions were not reciprocated or even well-received. Reciprocity is not simply a measurement of "this for that." It includes a mutual care and sympathy with the friend. We may be able to do nothing to mitigate our friend's suffering, but we can be present to them in their pain. The Jewish mourning ritual of sitting *shiva* is a prime example of "being with." During the first seven days after a death, friends visit the family of the deceased and offer their presence as consolation for their loss. The good of the other who is mutually concerned about your own good leads to the third characteristic that marks a true friendship: we are better people because of our friends.

Our true friendships evidence beneficence, mutuality/reciprocity, and betterment. Not every aspect will be equally in play at every moment of a relationship. Even friendships that originate in advantage or pleasure demonstrate these qualities to various degrees. The foundation of friendship relationships is a certain level playing field. But if Aquinas is right, and our goal in life is to become friends of God, how do we do that when we are most certainly not on a level playing field? A second question is, "why would God want to be our friend in the first place?"

The answer to both is actually quite simple, according to Aquinas. God desires our happiness, and the fullness of that happiness is expressed in friendship with God. It is initiated by grace, and witnesses to the divine friendship between Father and Son which is expressed in the Spirit of love. And it is a life activity to which God invites us. But as Aquinas recognized, we are at a bit of a disadvantage given our limited human nature. "Charity, as we have said, is our friendship for God arising from our sharing in eternal happiness, which is not a matter of natural goods but of gifts of grace."[15] The gift of grace transcends the gulf between the limitation of human beings and the incomprehensibility of the Divine. Grace helps to level the playing field.

Just so, as Aristotle noted, friendship requires a certain equality, and such is not possible with God. Aquinas answered this by explaining that our friendship with God is in part an analogy, a friendship *of a sort*. The fullness of our friendship with God is made complete by our union with God. Until then, our friendship is just at the beginning stages. As ethicist Paul Wadell notes, "What grace intends, charity achieves, this union of ourselves with God that is the harvest of a lifetime of friendship, of passionate seeking for God."[16]

This friendship love initiated by God, sustained by grace, and witnessed to by the Trinity, is the ultimate spiritual pursuit. The Scriptures are the Word of God, God's revelation to us about God's activities, desires, and hopes for God's people. As such, we should be able to search the Bible for examples of friendships that illuminate our path toward friendship with God.

The Bible as a Narrative of God's Friendship

Numerous examples of friendships are threaded throughout the Scriptures. For example, in the books of Exodus and Numbers, we meet Moses, Aaron, and Miriam, three siblings who remind us of our own family's blessings and squabbles. When the baby Moses is placed in a basket in the Nile River, his sister carefully keeps watch, and then offers to get a wet nurse for the baby when he is "found" by Pharaoh's daughter (Exodus 2:4). As an adult, Moses encounters God in a burning bush. God directs him to lead God's people out of slavery (chapters 3–4). But Moses admits he isn't a good speaker, so God sends Moses' brother Aaron to serve as the spokesperson. Together the brothers go to Pharaoh and eventually secure the release of the Hebrew slaves (chapters 5–13). And then after the miraculous crossing through the Red Sea, Miriam leads the women in song and dance: "Sing to the Lord, for he has triumphed gloriously; / horse and rider he has thrown into the sea!" (15:21).

Moses is the leader, Aaron a priest, and Miriam a prophet—three siblings who work together to realize God's plan for Israel. But forty years on the road is an exceedingly long journey. Along the way, Aaron bends to the will of the people and builds a golden calf which the people worship (Exodus chapter 32). Later both Miriam and Aaron grow jealous of Moses' relationship with God, so they complain that he had married a foreigner. In no uncertain terms, God sets them straight:

Hear my words: / When there are prophets among you, / I the LORD make myself known to them in visions; / I speak to them in dreams. / Not so with my servant Moses; / he is entrusted with all my house. / With him I speak face to face—clearly, not in riddles; / and he beholds the form of the LORD. / Why then were you not afraid to speak against my servant Moses? (Numbers 12:6-8)

God punishes Miriam, to the horror of Aaron, who begs Moses to intercede. "And Moses cried to the LORD, 'O God, please heal her'" (Numbers 12:13). These three may have had their disagreements along the way, but when put to the test, friendship and family win out.

The Book of Ruth is the story of a steadfast friendship born out of adversity. A novella sandwiched in our canon between Judges and First Samuel, Ruth is a tragedy turned to triumph because of the female characters who rely on their own ingenuity and love. When the story opens, Naomi has lost her husband and two grown sons. She dismisses her daughters-in-law, Orpah and Ruth, so that they may return to their own people. But Ruth recommits to her mother-in-law, even though she is legally freed from caring for her. She chooses to be an alien in a foreign land in order to accompany Naomi into a new life.

Do not press me to leave you / or to turn back from following you! / Where you go, I will go; / where you lodge, I will lodge; / your people shall be my people, / and your God my God. / Where you die, I will die— / there will I be buried. / May the LORD do thus and so to me, / and more as well, / if even death parts me from you! (Ruth 1:16-17)

After they arrive in Bethlehem, the two set about finding a spouse for Ruth so as to bring up children in the name of Ruth's deceased husband. Their faithfulness in adversity is well-rewarded. Ruth marries Boaz, and their son "Obed [became the father] of Jesse, and Jesse [became the father] of David" (Ruth 4:22).

The Bible also depicts friendships among comrades-in-arms, bosses and workers, and companions on the journey. The friendship of fellow soldiers David and Jonathan is forged under the weight of war and Saul's evil machinations. In First Samuel, Saul is anointed king over the people, but his kingship is wrought with personal demons and professional difficulties. David, a shepherd's son from the tiny village of Bethlehem, will rise from Saul's ranks and after Saul's death become the king of Israel. But before all that, we meet David and his friend Jonathan, the son of Saul (1 Samuel chapters 18–20).

The soul of Jonathan was bound to the soul of David, and Jonathan loved him as his own soul. . . . Then Jonathan made a covenant with David, because he loved him as his own soul. Jonathan stripped himself of the robe that he was wearing, and gave it to David, and his armor, and even his sword and his bow and his belt. (18:1,3-4)

Anyone who has served in the military knows the experience of comrades-in-arms. The very foundation of military service is trust in your fellow soldiers, leading to bonds of fraternity that extend years beyond one's enlistment. And so it would seem that Jonathan and David forge their friendship on the battlefield. But theirs is also a story of reversals. Jonathan, as Saul's son, is the heir to the throne, but he gives his symbols of power (robe, sword, and armor) to David, the son of a shepherd. Saul is enraged with jealousy over David's popularity and seeks to kill him. Despite Saul's disparaging treatment, Jonathan remains loyal and renews his covenant of friendship with David (20:42).

A twelfth-century Cistercian abbot by the name of Blessed Aelred reflected on this relationship in his *Treatise on Spiritual Friendship*, a medieval discussion of the virtues of friendship. Jonathan's fidelity to his friend is an example to emulate.

> 92. Jonathan alone, with more reason for envy, thought that his father should be opposed, that he should put himself at the service of his friend and offer advice in so great a crisis, because Jonathan set friendship above a kingdom. "You will be king," he said, "and I will be second after you."

> 93. Even when the king imposes the sentence of death on David, Jonathan does not fail his friend. . . . So maddened is the king at his words that he tries to pin Jonathan to the wall with his spear, adding abuse to his threats. . . .

94. Who would not be angered and aroused to envy by this taunt? Whose love, whose favor, whose abiding friendship would not be corrupted, weakened, and destroyed by it? But this youth, supreme in love, reverences the rights of friendship. Unflinching in the face of threats and unmoved by insults, unmindful of fame but mindful of kindness, he despises a kingdom for the sake of friendship. "You will be king," he says, "and I will be the second after you."...

96. Here was a genuine, perfect, stable, and lasting friendship, not spoiled by envy or weakened by suspicion or ruined by ambition. This friendship although so attacked, after such a battering, neither yielded nor collapsed. Though shaken in many a siege it proved unbending, and after many a wound and injury, it remained steadfast. Therefore, go and do likewise.[17]

Aelred's words remind us that the Bible's narratives of friendship are meant to inspire us. And divine inspiration seems to be the foundation of the relationship between the prophet Jeremiah and his scribe, Baruch. The lot of a prophet is a difficult one and Jeremiah frequently bemoans his calling (Jeremiah 1:4-10, 16:1-2, 20:7-18). During his forty-five years of prophetic ministry, Jeremiah attempts to bring the kingdom of Judah back into faithful worship of God before, during, and after the destruction of Jerusalem by Babylon in 586 BC While the invading armies are literally at the door, God instructs Jeremiah to purchase a piece of property now in the hands of the enemy. We are introduced to Baruch, son of Neriah, son of Mahseiah, to whom Jeremiah entrusts the deed to the property (32:12). In chapter 36, the Lord instructs Jeremiah to write down his prophecies. Jeremiah calls Baruch to serve as a scribe. Baruch is also to read the scroll in the Temple, because the prophet was barred from the sacred precincts. Baruch follows orders dutifully and reads the scroll.

> When [the officials] heard all the words, they turned to one another in alarm, and said to Baruch, "We certainly must report all these words to the king." Then they questioned Baruch, "Tell us now, how did you write all these words? Was it at his dictation?" Baruch answered them, "He dictated all these words to me, and I wrote them with ink on the scroll." Then the officials said to Baruch, "Go and hide, you and Jeremiah, and let no one know where you are." (36:16-19)

Befriending a prophet means bearing the ire of his enemies. The king burns the scroll piece by piece, so under Jeremiah's dictation Baruch writes a second one (36:32). When last seen, Baruch is accompanying his mentor and friend on his way to exile in Egypt (43:6). The deutero-canonical Book of Baruch presents the scribe as living in Babylon and writing to the exiles in the tradition of Jeremiah's preaching. Though likely not written by the historical Baruch, the book evidences that the tradition recognized the close ties between prophet and scribe.

First and Second Timothy present a similar portrait of friendship between the teacher and his disciple. These two second-century AD letters written in the name of Paul but long after his death read like Paul's last will and testament. In the voice of the aged and imprisoned Paul, we hear Paul's words of direction and encouragement to his pro-tégé, Timothy (1 Timothy 1:1-2). Timothy is instructed to fight the good fight against heretical teaching (1 Timothy 1:18-19), and to fan into a flame the gift of God given to him by the imposition of Paul's hands (2 Timothy 1:6). Paul longs for Timothy's visit, not simply because Timothy can bring Paul's cloak and the books and writing materi-als he needs (2 Timothy 4:13), but because Paul has deep affection for his "beloved child" whom he holds in prayer (1:2-3). "Recalling your tears, I long to see you so that I may be filled with joy" (2 Timothy 1:4).

As evident in the relationship between Paul and Timothy, a shared purpose often forms the foundation for friendship. Similarly, a common journey unites and strengthens the bonds between Mary and Elizabeth. In their encounter, we see true friendship where they do good, share mutually, and seek the welfare of each other. After her own angelic annunciation, Mary learns about her rela-tive Elizabeth's pregnancy (Luke 1:36). Mary then travels in haste to the hill country of Judah (Luke 1:39). The word we translate as "haste," *spoudē* in Greek, is found only three times in the New Testament (here, Mark 6:25, and

2 Corinthians 8:8). While it has the meaning of hurried activity, it can also signal earnestness. Paul writes to the Corinthians that "I am testing the genuineness of your love against the earnestness [*spoudē*] of others (2 Cor inthians 8:8)." Mary's hurried trip to see Elizabeth is often read as Mary's need to share her good (or difficult) news with someone who would understand. But Mary's own declaration that she is the handmaid of the Lord (Luke 1:38) suggests that Mary's haste stems from her earnest desire to attend to her older cousin during her pregnancy. And the feeling is mutual. Upon Mary's arrival, Elizabeth is filled with the Holy Spirit (1:41) just as Mary was (1:35). Both women sing songs of praise; Elizabeth sings of Mary's faith in God (1:45), and Mary sings the praises of God:

> My spirit rejoices in God my Savior, / for he has looked with favor on the lowliness of his servant. / Surely, from now on all generations will call me blessed. (1:47-48)

Mary remains with Elizabeth for the duration of the latter's pregnancy (1:56), during which time we can imagine that both women took comfort in their shared experience of God's miraculous grace. They were living proof of the angel's words: "For nothing will be impossible with God" (1:37).

That profound trust in God's promises undergirds the friendship among Jesus and three siblings, Mary, Martha, and Lazarus. As the Gospel of John tells us, the sisters send for Jesus because their brother whom Jesus loves is ill (John

11:3). By the time Jesus arrives, Lazarus has been dead for four days. Martha goes out to meet Jesus and says, "Lord, if you had been here, my brother would not have died" (11:21). Certainly, Martha is acknowledging Jesus' unique relationship with God (11:22), but we can also hear anger and disappointment that Jesus, their dear friend, had not been with them in their suffering. Mary echoes Martha's sentiments when Jesus arrives at the tomb (11:32). Standing before the tomb of his friend, amidst the wailing of mourners, Jesus weeps, and those gathered around acknowledge, "See how he loved him!" (11:36). Jesus calls Lazarus out of the tomb and back to life, and so proves his words to Martha, "I am the resurrection and the life. Those who believe in me, even though they die, will live" (11:25). The raising of Lazarus stands as the seventh sign that witnesses to Jesus' true identity as God's Son, but on another level, it also confirms Jesus' humanity. Jesus had friends, loved those friends, and wept at their loss. We can relate. So we are not surprised when later in the Gospel of John, Jesus calls his own disciples "friends" (15:15).

But despite these narrative examples, the actual word for "friend"—*re'a* in the Hebrew or *philos* in the Greek—occurs only a couple hundred times in the Bible and is found mostly in a collection of writings we call Wisdom Literature (Job, Psalms, Proverbs, Ecclesiastes, Song of Songs, Wisdom, and Ben Sira). These books are unique in their theological perspective. As New Testament scholar Barbara Bowe has noted, Wisdom Literature presents God's revelation not primarily in historical events but in the ordinariness of life.[18] It is in the marketplace that God is to be found, among the mundane human concerns of everyday. Ancient Near Eastern wisdom emphasized attentive observation and reflection on lived experience so as to discern the best way to be successful. The goal of such wisdom was practical. How are we to live, love, and prosper in light of the vicissitudes of life? In our understanding, we would view Wisdom Literature as "how-to books on becoming and remaining successful in God's ordered world." So in light of Wisdom Literature's particular concern with the everydayness of life, we are not surprised that friendship enters into the discussion of right living. Let's look at some examples.

The Book of Job is a narrative about why bad things happen to good people. It stands as a critique to standard Wisdom theology, which held that if you obeyed God you were rewarded. If you didn't, you suffered. The story of Job is about a good and righteous man who is tested by God. Throughout the narrative, Job's three friends who ascribe to Wisdom theology seek to uncover what Job did wrong. After his friend Eliphaz's critique, Job laments his situation:

> In truth I have no help in me, / and any resource is driven from me. / Those who withhold kindness from a friend / forsake the fear of the Almighty. / My companions are treacherous like a torrent-bed, / like freshets that pass away. (Job 6:13-15)

Lament was a common way to give voice to the frustration, fear, and deep depression of those in dire situations.

Psalm 55 is a lament in which the writer has been betrayed by his friends and prays that God punish the oath breakers.

> Give ear to my prayer, O God; / do not hide yourself from my supplication. / Attend to me, and answer me; / I am troubled in my complaint. / I am distraught by the noise of the enemy, / because of the clamor of the wicked. / For they bring trouble upon me, / and in anger they cherish enmity against me. /. . . It is not enemies who taunt me— / I could bear that; / it is not adversaries who deal insolently with me— / I could hide from them. / But it is you, my equal, / my companion, my familiar friend, / with whom I kept pleasant company; / we walked in the house of God with the throng. (Psalm 55:1-3,12-14)

Psalm 15 depicts the behavior one should expect of one's friend:

> O LORD, who may abide in your tent? / Who may dwell on your holy hill? / Those who walk blamelessly, and do what is right, / and speak the truth from their heart; / who do not slander with their tongue, / and do no evil to their friends, / nor take up a reproach against their neighbors. (Psalm 15:1-3)

Thus the Psalmist upholds a high view of friendship that we have seen thus far elsewhere in the Bible and in antiquity.

The Book of Proverbs is a collection of sayings designed to guide the wise along the path to success and moral rectitude. This biblical collection of proverbial sayings is distinguished from other ancient sapiential texts by its belief that "fear of the LORD" (Proverbs 1:7) is the source of wisdom.

> My child, keep my words / and store up my commandments with you; / keep my commandments and live, / keep my teachings as the apple of your eye; / bind them on your fingers, / write them on the tablet of your heart. / Say to wisdom, "You are my sister," / and call insight your intimate friend. (7:1-4)

Friends are foundational to success, so Proverbs notes, "A friend loves at all times, / and kinsfolk are born to share adversity" (17:17). But not all friends are equal: "Some friends play at friendship / but a true friend sticks closer than one's nearest kin" (18:24) and "Many seek the favor of the generous, / and everyone is a friend to a giver of gifts" (19:6). Proverbs also proposes that one's friendship extends to one's family:

> Do not forsake your friend or the friend of your parent; / do not go to the house of your kindred in the day of your calamity. / Better is a neighbor who is nearby / than kindred who are far away. (27:10)

While the Book of Proverbs offers pithy sayings on the topic, the most developed discussion on friendship in the Wisdom Literature is found in the Book of Ben Sira (Sirach). Writing in the second century BC, Ben Sira attempts to counter the influence of Hellenism (Greek culture) by reminding the Jews of his day that the traditions of Israel, and not Greek philosophy and culture, are the foundations of true wisdom. He appears familiar with the Aristotelian tenets of friendship and recognizes three different types of friend. The first, which Aristotle would call a friendship of advantage, Ben Sira names as "friends who are such when it suits them" (Sirach 6:8). They sup at your table, and when things go well they are your "second self" (6:11). But when adversity comes, they quickly depart (6:12). Another type of friend is in reality an enemy. "And there are friends who change into enemies, / and tell of the quarrel to your disgrace" (6:9). The truest form of a friend, whom Aristotle would call a virtuous friend, Ben Sira names as the faithful friend (6:14). These not only support you and stand by you, but also accompany you in your quest for God.

> Faithful friends are a sturdy shelter: / whoever finds one has found a treasure. / Faithful friends are beyond price; / no amount can balance their worth. / Faithful friends are life-saving medicine; / and those who fear the Lord / will find them. / Those who fear the Lord direct their friendship aright, / for as they are, so are their neighbors also. (6:14-17)

These faithful friends teach us how to be a better friend. The word for "faithful" is *pistos* in the Greek and also means trustworthy or believing. But in the context that Sirach describes, a better translation might be "loyal." Faithful friends are loyal. In Hebrew, the word most often translated for "loyal" is *hesed*, an attribute first given to God. As Brother John Barker, OFM, notes:

> *Hesed* is to be grounded in God's fidelity and commitment to relationship. As one of my students recently put it, "*hesed* looks like mercy on the outside, but on the inside, it is fidelity." The word and the reality point to the absolute devotion, faithfulness, and commitment of God to those with whom God is in relationship.[19]

God's *hesed*, or loyal faithfulness based on the covenant with the chosen people, toward us points us in the direction of how we should behave with others, most especially our friends.

In four other sections (9:10-16, 11:29–12:18, 22:19-26, and 26:28–27:21), Ben Sira also discusses friendship, the number of occurrences suggesting the importance of the relationship. He offers practical advice on maintaining faithful friends. Old friends are to be cherished, like fine wine, he writes: "Do not abandon old friends, / for new ones cannot equal them. / A new friend is like new wine; / when it has aged, you can drink it with pleasure" (Sirach 9:10). If you are a true friend, you offer correction when necessary. According to Ben Sira:

> Question a friend; perhaps he did not do it; / or
> if he did, so that he may not do it again. / . . .
> Question a friend, for often it is slander; / so do
> not believe everything you hear. / A person may
> make a slip without intending it. / Who has not
> sinned with his tongue? (19:13,15-16)

But there are limits to one's friendship.

> One who throws a stone at birds scares them
> away, / and one who reviles a friend destroys a
> friendship. / Even if you draw your sword against
> a friend, / do not despair, for there is a way back.
> / If you open your mouth against your friend, /
> do not worry, for reconciliation is possible. / But
> as for reviling, arrogance, disclosure of secrets, or
> a treacherous blow— / in these cases any friend
> will take to flight. (22:20-22)

The practical advice of Wisdom Literature is no less valuable today. But as the concept developed in biblical and world history, friendship also had political connotations. Known as "apocrypha" or deuterocanonical texts in the Protestant canon, the books of First and Second Maccabees recount the resistance by religious Jews to Hellenistic rule and its legislation against Jewish practices in the second century BC. In First Maccabees, the Jews are engaged in a letter-writing campaign in order to solicit support in their fight to free themselves from Syrian tyrants. "Now when Jonathan [the Maccabean Jewish military leader] saw that the time was favorable for him, he chose men and sent them to Rome to confirm and renew the friendship with them" (1 Maccabees 12:1). These political "friendships" set up alliances, but ones that were often unequal. The stronger became the patron. The weaker became the client who owed obeisance to the patron. This seems to be the case in the Gospel of John where Pilate is accused of not being "a friend of Caesar" because he wishes to release Jesus (John 19:12). Pilate owed his appointment to the emperor and if he wished to progress along the political circuit, he needed to appease his boss. A visible demonstration of his "friendship" with Caesar is a fragment of a dedicatory inscription which states that Pontius Pilate erected a temple to Tiberius's honor. Found in Caesarea Maritima, Pilate's headquarters, the reconstructed inscription reads, "Pontius Pilate the prefect of Judea has dedicated to the people of Caesarea a temple in honor of Tiberius."

When we turn to the New Testament, we see that the apostle Paul frequently uses friendship language and images to convey his relationship with believers and their relationship with Christ. In Philippians, Paul addresses a beloved community of Gentile believers living in a thoroughly Roman city in northeastern Greece. In this letter, we find the ten expressions of friendship language common in Greek rhetoric. These include affection (1:8), partnership (1:5,7, 2:1, 3:10, 4:15), unity of soul or spirit (1:27, 2:20, 1:27), like-mindedness (2:2, 4:2), yoke-mate/true companion (4:3), giving and receiving (4:15), common struggles and joys (1:30, 3:18), absence/presence (1:27, 2:12,24), virtue friendship (4:8,13,19) and moral paradigm (3:17, 4:8-9).

Paul "transforms the meaning and experience of friendship by redefining each of the essential ideas of friendship given by Hellenistic essays on friendship in terms of communion with Christ and empowerment by Christ."[20] Likely, Paul's own experience led to his deep appreciation of the gift and value of friendship, for the Philippians held a special place in his heart for the help they offered him during his sojourn among them and when he needed assistance (1:19, 4:14).

Conclusion

Though written nearly 2,500 years ago, Aristotle's definition of a friend still holds true. We know we have a true friend, one whom Aristotle calls "virtuous," because he or she demonstrates beneficence by doing good for us and with us. A friend is also one with whom we are mutual and reciprocal. It's not all on me to uphold the friendship. And finally, a friend makes us better. He or she calls us to be our best selves, often seeing in us possibilities we cannot see in ourselves.

Thomas Aquinas ups the ante, so to speak, when he proposes that our goal in this Christian life is to become friends with God. Our ultimate happiness resides in our pursuit of this divine relationship. So we should not be surprised that our Scriptures have much to say about friendship. Whether personal, familial, political, or communal, the biblical portrayals of friendship mirror for us what friendship with God might be like.

Now let's go home. Let's turn to questions about the friends in our lives and how we might find Scriptural support as we, too, endeavor to become friends of God.

For Reflection:

- How do you define friendship? Of the Scripture passages cited in this chapter, which one most speaks to your experience of friendship?

- Have you experienced the three types of friendship that Aristotle describes: utilitarian, pleasure-seeking, and virtuous?

p. 23

Friendship is a bond between 2 people who show an unconditional love for one another.

Jonathan and David
Mary and Elizabeth

Chapter Two

Can I Be Friends with my Kids?: Exploring Jesus' Relationship with His Family

Introduction

On the corner of State Street and Washington Avenue, Marshall Field's department store stood as an icon of old Chicago. For generations, a magnificently decorated tree was the centerpiece of the store's restaurant, The Walnut Room, where holiday shoppers would dine before or after their Christmas shopping. Annually, my friend Dennis would take his daughter for lunch under the tree before they began their Christmas shopping for his wife. It was a father-daughter ritual that managed to survive the surly teen years and even the years away at college. No matter the exigencies of their lives, lunch in The Walnut Room remained. That is, until the company closed in 2005, and the family ritual had to be revised. When parents ponder whether they can be friends with their adult children, I think of Dennis and his daughter Megan, sitting under the festooned three-story evergreen. It seems to me that the dividends of friendship accrue from a lifetime of small deposits into a bank of love and relationship. But with true friendship, along with doing good for the other and seeking their betterment, there must exist a mutuality between each individual. While the first two certainly characterize a parent's care for their child, the third, mutuality or reciprocity, seems outside the appropriate boundaries of the familial relationship. Let's see what light Scripture might shine on our topic.

Love Your Children; Honor Your Parents

According to our Scriptures the two primary responsibilities of parents are to care for their children (Psalm 103:13) and to teach their children to walk in God's ways (Deuteronomy 11:19 and Psalm 78:5). And in response,

> [Children] are indeed a heritage from the LORD, / the fruit of the womb a reward. / Like arrows in the hand of a warrior / are the [children] of one's youth. / Happy is the man who has / his quiver full of them. (Psalm 127:3-5)

For their part, children are to "Honor your father and your mother, so that your days may be long in the land that the LORD your God is giving you" (Exodus 20:12). Children who honor their parents will then find joy in their children (Sirach 3:5). The Hebrew word translated as "honor" means "weighty" and came to refer to those persons in positions of responsibility. The same root word is related to "glory" and refers to God's presence. The commandment clearly notes that children owe their parents respect as befitting their parents' positions of authority and responsibility.

But the Scriptures consider the whole of one's life, so that while a parent may care for the child when he or she is young, the roles will later be reversed.

> My child, help your father in his old age, / and do not grieve him as long as he lives; / even if his mind fails, be patient with him; / because you have all your faculties do not despise him. / For kindness to a father will not be forgotten, / and will be credited to you against your sins. (Sirach 3:12-14)

Likewise, in the New Testament, mutuality and reciprocity are evident when both parent and child act according to their prescribed roles.

> Children, obey your parents in the Lord, for this is right. "Honor your father and mother"—this is the first commandment with a promise: "so that it may be well with you and you may live long on the earth." And, fathers, do not provoke your children to anger, but bring them up in the discipline and instruction of the Lord. (Ephesians 6:1-4)

Our definition of friendship describes a relationship in which both "friends" demonstrate beneficence toward each other, become better people, and share a level of mutuality and reciprocity in the process. Our Scriptures clearly recognize that the respect and care parents and children display to each other alters over time, so that mutuality and reciprocity indeed can be significant aspects of the relationship between parents and adult children.

What Would Jesus Do?

According to Saul Olyan, family and friends in the Old Testament share some common characteristics and obligations: a duty to be loving, loyal, and supportive (particularly during adversity), and trustworthiness.[21] But there were also separate expectations for family members. For example, a family member had to act as a redeemer if another family member was sold into slavery (Leviticus 25:49). If a husband died without leaving an heir, his brother was to marry his widow and raise up children in his brother's name (known as levirate marriage; Genesis 38:8). Finally, one of the most significant responsibilities for families was the burial of their deceased members (Genesis 47:30).

This tradition of responsibilities and expectations for family and friends is also depicted in our New Testament texts, though adapted for a different historical period. Friends could impose on their neighbors for help (Luke 11:5-6). The Sadducees asked Jesus about levirate marriage: "In the resurrection, then, whose wife of the seven will she be? For all of them had married her" (Matthew 22:28). When invited to follow Jesus, a would-be disciple announces that he must first bury his father (Matthew 8:21).

While the Scriptures do not name a relationship between parent and child as a friendship per se, we can draw such inferences by carefully reading the narratives in light of our definition of friendship: doing good, betterment, and mutuality. In this light, perhaps the most poignant Scriptural example of friendship between a parent and a child is found in the narratives about Jesus and his mother, Mary, to which we now turn.

Doing Good

All three synoptic Gospels include the story of Jesus' encounter with his family (Mark 3:20-35, Matthew 12:46-50, Luke 8:19-21). In Mark's account, Jesus returns "home" to Capernaum and is so pressed by the crowd that he and his disciples are unable even to eat. The text then reads, "When his family heard it, they went out to restrain him, for people were saying, 'He has gone out of his mind'" (Mark 3:21). The Greek word, *existēmi*, has the metaphorical connotation of "to be out of one's wits." A more modern vernacular translation might be to say, "He is crazy." It's unclear if the "people" who think he is out of his mind are his family members or the crowd.

While his family is making their way to Jesus, scribes who have come from Jerusalem accuse him of being possessed by Beelzebul, a roundabout expression for Satan. The charge is that Jesus is able to cast out demons because he is in league with them. To this illogical claim, Jesus responds: "If a kingdom is divided against itself, that kingdom cannot stand. And if a house is divided against itself, that house will not be able to stand" (Mark 3:24-25).

At root the challenge is to the origin of Jesus' authority. Not by an evil spirit is Jesus able to conquer the evil realm, but by the power of the Holy Spirit. To cast aspersions on this source of power is unforgiveable. In a pronouncement beginning with the solemn expression, "Truly I tell you," Jesus draws a line in the sand. All sins will be forgiven, save the sin against the Holy Spirit, for "whoever blasphemes against the Holy Spirit can never have forgiveness, but is guilty of an eternal sin" (Mark 3:29). On the heels of this announcement, his mother and his brothers arrive and stand outside. Word reaches Jesus:

> "'Your mother and your brothers and sisters are outside, asking for you.' And he replied, 'Who are my mother and my brothers?' And looking at those who sat around him, he said, 'Here are my mother and my brothers! Whoever does the will of God is my brother and sister and mother.'"
> (Mark 3:32-35)

I can only imagine how my mother would have responded to me if I had casually dismissed her arrival and called those surrounding me my new family! We are not told how the family of Jesus responded, or how they felt about Jesus extending his "family" to include those around him. What is clear is that here Jesus is changing the definition of family, which will have implications for the later evangelizing mission of the Church. After the death and resurrection of Jesus, the apostles will continue Jesus' preaching ministry. Any who do the will of God and believe in Jesus Christ will be invited into the community, opening the way for the Gentiles.

To understand what motivates Jesus' family, we need to turn back time. In the first-century Mediterranean world, the most important social value was family honor. The family is the first and primary experience of love and safety. The family protects its members. Jesus' family have heard rumors, and they are worried about him. But the family is also concerned with its corporate status. Honor and shame are the two poles that regulated status in the ancient world. Members of the family were to bring honor to the family and avoid bringing shame. Not only is Jesus unable to eat, but some people are suggesting that he is out of his mind, and the scribes deride him as being in league with Satan. No wonder they hurried to Capernaum!

And despite the distance and lack of modern modes of communication, folks knew to whom Jesus belonged. The Gospel of John notes that a crowd also commented, "Is not this Jesus, the son of Joseph, whose father and mother we know?" (John 6:42). Likewise, in Matthew, Jesus' own hometown questions his ability: "Is not this the carpenter's son? Is not his mother called Mary? And are not his brothers James and Joseph and Simon and Judas? And are not all his sisters with us? Where then did this man get all this?" (Matthew 13:55-56).

So, if Jesus' family has come to the rescue in order to preserve his and their honor and to avoid shame, why is Jesus leaving them at the door, so to speak? Perhaps

Jesus isn't turning away from his family, but away from their concerns about proper behavior and societal rules. Jesus counters that a true member of his family is the one who does the will of God. Jesus expands the concept of family so that it is no longer limited to blood or marriage ties. Doing good for one another extends beyond familial relationships.

Betterment

The story of the wedding feast at Cana in John 2:1-11 could also be read through the lens of honor and shame. The mother of Jesus (she is never named in John's Gospel) is concerned that the celebration will be ruined, and shame will be cast upon the groom's family if the wine runs out. Without hesitating, she informs Jesus of this predicament, "They have no wine" (2:3). Mirroring his reaction to his family's sudden arrival as discussed above, Jesus responds, "Woman, what concern is that to you and to me? My hour has not yet come" (2:4). Throughout John's Gospel, the mention of his "hour" refers to Jesus' glorification, his return to the Father (13:1). Jesus seems to be saying not that he isn't able but that he isn't ready to reveal his glory.

But his mother knows otherwise. She turns to the servants and states, "Do whatever he tells you" (John 2:5). We know how this story ends. Water becomes the finest wine, and the groom is none the wiser. Because of his mother's encouragement, Jesus demonstrates the first sign of his true identity, and as a result, "his disciples believed in him" (2:11).

Like the mother of Jesus, parents most often know what is best for their children, even if their children don't like it. When, at age 11, Aiden lost his mom, he, his sister, and his dad were absolutely bereft. The next football season, Aiden refused to try out, preferring to immerse himself in video games. His dad, Kevin, also one of the coaches, encouraged, cajoled, and finally commanded that he play. Begrudgingly Aidan donned his pads and entered the fray. And the grieving little boy came alive again. He needed a team; he needed to belong; he needed to be pushed beyond his self-imposed limits. As with the mother of Jesus, Aiden's dad knew what his son needed. It will be years before father and son enjoy the maturity of friendship, but its seeds are planted in every moment that the parent encourages the betterment of his child.

Mutuality

All the Gospels narrate that the women followers of Jesus witnessed his execution, but only the Gospel of John clearly identifies that Jesus' mother is among them. "Standing near the cross of Jesus were his mother, and his mother's sister, Mary the wife of Clopas, and Mary Magdalene" (John 19:25). We might ponder: how does the crucifixion of Jesus look through his mother's eyes? She has done good for him, she has called forth his true potential, and now at the foot of the cross, she experiences mutuality in shared suffering and shame.

It is likely hard for us to imagine the suffering, the pain, the seeming cruelty of it all. We wear crosses around our neck as jewelry. We bless ourselves with the Sign of the Cross. We hang crucifixes on our walls. We have totally lost the sense of the horror of this brutal act of capital punishment. A modern comparison would be to place a model of an electric chair on your wall or around your neck. That's repulsive. So was the crucifixion. And watching it all is his mother.

Pilate had a sign placed above Jesus that read "Jesus of Nazareth, the King of the Jews." "Many of the Jews read this inscription, because the place where Jesus was crucified was near the city; and it was written in Hebrew, in Latin, and in Greek" (John 19:20). If she could read, would Mary have affirmed this title? Yes, Jesus of Nazareth, she could acknowledge, and a flood of memories would overwhelm her. The majority of Jesus' life (John's Gospel suggests at least twenty-seven years) would have been spent in Nazareth and its environs. But "King of the Jews"—that was the accusation leveled against her Son. Never in the Gospel accounts does Jesus claim the title for himself. Staring up at a sign she can barely read and hardly understand, Mary would see only "Jesus, my Son, a victim."

When Jesus saw his mother and the disciple whom he loved standing beside her, he said to his mother, "Woman, here is your son." Then he said to the disciple, "Here is your mother." And from that hour the disciple took her into his own home. (19:26-27)

As he had done at the wedding in Cana, Jesus calls his mother, "Woman." Renowned biblical scholar Father Raymond E. Brown proposed that this was Jesus' polite term for addressing women, as evident elsewhere in the Gospels. Whatever Jesus' intent, we are struck at the distance the word creates. He does not use a term of endearment or of personal relationship. Rather, he identifies her by her biology: woman. And by doing so, Jesus has opened up the possibility for all women (and I would argue men as well) to find their place in this encounter. Those who stand on the verge of absolute grief, seemingly unredeemable suffering, and facing an uncertain and frightening future are themselves standing as "Woman" or "Man" at the foot of his cross.

"Here is your son" (John 19:26). Jesus is not being self-referential. He is giving his mother a new son. And to this disciple whom Jesus loved, he is giving a new mother. New relationships are born from the experience of grief. Mary does not cease to be a mother at the death of her Son Jesus. But she must now learn to be "mother" and "woman" in a new way. Perhaps Jesus was preparing her for this new role when he exclaimed, "Here are my mother and my brothers! Whoever does the will of God is my brother and sister and mother" (Mark 3:34b-35).

Conclusion

And so we return to family. In Mark chapter 3, Jesus had invited others into the family of God, and here Jesus unites his beloved disciple and his mother in a new relationship of shared grief. Throughout his life, Jesus was being "befriended" by his mother as she did good for him, called forth his own unique qualities, and now shared in this profound moment of suffering. Given our narratives about Jesus and his family, we should not be surprised that the one present at his birth would be standing with him at his death.

As our Scriptures present it, becoming friends with our adult children is not something that suddenly occurs. Rather, as with any friendship, it takes times, testing, perseverance, and a mutual experience of doing good for each other so that both parent and child live into their full potential.

For Reflection:

- Spend some time reflecting on these encounters in the Gospels in light of your own experiences with honor and shame in your family of origin.

- Reflect on your relationships with your adult children (or with your parents). How might you develop a more mutual friendship? What qualities do you think are necessary?

Chapter Three

Is My Spouse Also My Friend?: Life after the Honeymoon

Introduction

Not many times throughout my life as a Catholic religious sister have I thought wistfully about what life would have been like if I had chosen to get married. But I do remember that a spontaneous outing for ice cream gave me pause.

Michael and Pat were our married neighbors living across the hall during graduate school. We three were doing doctoral studies in Scripture, and the religious sister with whom I lived was in law school. All of that is to say that we kept odd hours, and exam time was particularly stressful. One snowy evening when we were all studying together, Pat had had enough of ancient texts. She turned to her husband and said, "I'd love some ice cream." With that Mike got up, put on his coat, and went to the store for ice cream. Did I mention it was snowing?

"Do they do that?" I asked Pat incredulously. "Do husbands just go out on cold, dark nights for frozen dessert because you asked?" Truly I began to rethink my vocation!

She laughed, mostly at my naiveté. "Yes, married life is all about who gets the ice cream for whom!"

Throughout our coursework, I had many opportunities to observe this young couple. Indeed, not all days were filled with ice cream, but they were certainly filled with love. Mike and Pat had begun their relationship as friends, and their married life became an intimate extension of that first relationship.

Because our Church is often seen as equating marriage with family, we tend to overlook the primary relationship that must first exist between the spouses. While the biblical world operated a bit differently when it came to marriage, our Scriptures still offer insight into how couples today might remain friends throughout their marriage.

A Relationship of Duty

The background of the Old Testament texts is the ancient Near Eastern world where marriages among rulers were alliances of power and not the products of love. King Solomon's seven hundred wives are an exaggerated example, though the Bible does say that Solomon loved them (1 Kings 11:3). Among the rank and file, marriages were arranged between clan members (Genesis 24:4), and marrying an outsider had dire consequences (Genesis chapter 34, Deuteronomy 7:2-5, Ezra 9:12). Marital metaphors are often used to describe God's relationship with Israel (Isaiah 54:5, 62:4-5; Jeremiah 3:14, 31:31-33; Ezekiel 16:8). And Hosea uses his unfaithful wife as an example of how God will stand by Israel, despite its infidelity (Hosea 2:16).

In the New Testament, Greco-Roman expectations mingled with those of first-century Judaism. Men tended to marry in their early thirties to girls in their late teens. Since the father of the house had ultimate authority, he arranged marriages for his sons that would benefit the family interests.[22] The right to divorce established by both Roman and Jewish law was challenged by Jesus (Mark 10:3-8). Some of the later New Testament letters attempt to integrate societal expectations with Christian morality, so they largely follow Greco-Roman patterns for how husbands and wives should behave (for example, see Colossians 3:18-25 and Titus 2:1-10).

Only occasionally do we glimpse an actual relationship between a husband and wife. Perhaps the most significant is Joseph's discovery of Mary's pregnancy and his unwillingness to put her to shame (Matthew 1:18-25). We have to dig a little deeper into our Scriptures to find examples of couples who seem to have built their relationship on friendship.

A Marriage of Promise

Though the story of Abraham and Sarah is set more than 4,000 years ago, much of the trials and tribulations of their marriage could be mapped onto today's couples. Inspired by a God only Abraham knows, he takes his wife and nephew and sets off to make his mark in the world (Genesis 12:1-5). Despite their desire, the couple remains childless (15:20).

God's three-fold promise of land, offspring, and blessing seems but a pipe dream. In fact, several times the promise is nearly extinguished. No sooner is the divine pledge given than Abraham jeopardizes everything by going to Egypt, where he passes Sarah off as his sister and she is taken into the harem of Pharaoh (12:11-16).

Sarah's barrenness was another obstacle to the fulfillment of the promise of numerous progeny (Genesis 11:30, 16:1). When Abraham and Sarah were too old for childbearing, God reiterated the promise, changing Sarai's name to Sarah, a variant of Sarai. Both forms mean "princess." As with Abraham (17:5), the name change from Abram is symbolic, representing a special destiny: "I will bless her, and moreover I will give you a son by her. I will bless her, and she shall give rise to nations; kings of peoples shall come from her" (17:16). Not surprisingly, Abraham's reaction to this news is laughter (17:17). Later it will be Sarah who laughs when she overhears their mysterious visitors inform Abraham that she would bear a son (18:1-15). Finally, the long-awaited heir is born to Sarah and Abraham, and appropriately, they name him Isaac, meaning "laughter" (21:1-8).

Sarah died at age 127, not yet having seen the promise made to her husband that their offspring would be as numerous as the stars and that this land in which they sojourned would become their own (Genesis chapter 15). Abraham, well up in age himself, performs the customary mourning rites for her. In the ancient Near East, as was true elsewhere, great rituals surrounded the death of a family member, especially the matriarch. The space that Sarah once occupied within the household had to be acknowledged and commemorated. She was irreplaceable. "Abraham went in to mourn for Sarah and to weep for her" (23:2).

We have to read between the lines to draw out what must have been a long and tumultuous friendship. Twice Abraham tries to pass Sarah off as his sister to avoid being killed (Genesis 12:11-18, 20:1-13). For her part, Sarah wants Abraham's son, Ishmael, to be killed to prevent his taking the birthright of her son Isaac (21:9-10). Both laugh at the plans and promises of God (17:17, 18:11-12). Likely Sarah was not laughing when Abraham returned after his near-sacrifice of the long-awaited son Isaac (22:9-14). Forgiveness, tenacity, and hope must have characterized their sixty-two years of journeying together.

In fact, aren't these the hallmarks of any healthy enduring marriage? Certainly, my friend, Gina, would say so. Friends often compliment her for having such a caring, considerate, and charming husband, especially when he is compared to their own husbands. "You should have chosen better!" she answers. Gina married her friend who then became her husband. After fifty years of marriage, both will admit that along the way of marriage you learn what battles to fight and what really isn't worth the anger. Friendship makes us better than we are, and Gina and Steve's marriage has become a public witness to the power of love and fidelity that is founded on friendship.

"Arise, my friend, my beautiful one, and come"

Where the story of Abraham and Sarah is about hope, faith, and trust for the long haul, Song of Songs speaks of the spark of passion between young lovers. Very early on, both Jewish and Christian traditions read Song of Songs through an allegorical lens: here is God yearning for Israel, or Christ desiring the Church. It represents a union between Christ and the individual's soul. The passion between lovers was the strongest image our ancestors in the faith had to convey God's pursuit of us.

What we call Song of Songs, also known as Song of Solomon (or Canticle of Canticles), is a series of love poems written in perhaps the third century BC and incorrectly attributed to Solomon. Organized into eight chapters, Song of Songs shares elements with ancient Egyptian romance poems and even cultic "marriage songs" from ancient Mesopotamia. The metaphors used to describe the physique of the young lovers are drawn from nature, yet they don't necessarily match our understanding of beauty. Known as *wasfs*, from the Arabic word for "description," these verbal portraits proceed from head to toe or vice versa. To appreciate the imagery, you have to first imagine "a flock of goats, / moving down the slopes of Gilead" (Song of Songs 4:1, 6:5). Seen from a distance, they become a strand of black flowing down a pale hillside. Now take the metaphorical leap and imagine a woman's hair as waves of black trailing down her shoulders. Likewise, the male lover's hair is described like palm fronds (5:11). A date palm can have 125 fronds, each thick and overlapping. We are to imagine a thick head of hair "black as a raven."

In Song of Songs, we have explicit mention of the beloved as "friend." The woman is thus identified eight times (Song 1:15, 2:2,10,13, 4:1,7. 5:2, 6:4). The man uses it as his preferred term for his beloved. Song of Songs expresses three powerful aspects of that friendship: presence, attraction, and strength of desire.

Presence

My beloved speaks and says to me: / "Arise, my love, my fair one, / and come away; / for now the winter is past, / the rain is over and gone. / The flowers appear on the earth; / the time of singing has come, / and the voice of the turtledove / is heard in our land. / The fig tree puts forth its figs, / and the vines are in blossom; / they give forth fragrance. / Arise, my love, my fair one, / and come away." (2:10-13)

Attraction

How beautiful you are, my love, / how very beautiful! / Your eyes are doves / behind your veil. / Your hair is like a flock of goats, / moving down the slopes of Gilead. / Your teeth are like a flock of shorn ewes / that have come up from the washing, / all of which bear twins, / and not one among them is bereaved. / Your lips are like a crimson thread, / and your mouth is lovely. / Your cheeks are like halves of a pomegranate / behind your veil. / Your neck is like the tower of David, / built in courses; / on it hang a thousand bucklers, / all of them shields of warriors. / Your two breasts are like two fawns, / twins of a gazelle, / that feed among the lilies. / Until the day breathes / and the shadows flee, / I will hasten to the mountain of myrrh / and the hill of frankincense. / You are altogether beautiful, my love; / there is no flaw in you. (4:1-7)

In chapter 5 of the Song, the woman describes her attraction to her beloved.

My beloved is all radiant and ruddy, / distinguished among ten thousand. / His head is the finest gold; / his locks are wavy, / black as a raven. / His eyes are like doves / beside springs of water, / bathed in milk, / fitly set. / His cheeks are like beds of spices, / yielding fragrance. / His lips are lilies, / distilling liquid myrrh. / His arms are rounded gold, / set with jewels. / His body is ivory work, / encrusted with sapphires. / His legs are alabaster columns, / set upon bases of gold. / His appearance is like Lebanon, / choice as the cedars. / His speech is most sweet, / and he is altogether desirable. / This is my beloved and this is my friend, / O daughters of Jerusalem. (5:10-16)

Strength of Desire

Several times this warning is repeated: "I adjure you, O daughters of Jerusalem, / . . . do not stir up or awaken love / until it is ready!" (2:7, 3:5, 8:4).

Song of Songs describes the importance of being physically present and how we see beauty in those we love. But it also warns that one should approach the passion of intimacy with care.

The Power of Passion

Song of Songs might seem an odd choice for a reflection on marriage and friendship. It speaks of desire, longing, and seeking the beloved. It seems overly intimate and personal. It's an encounter that should remain private. And yet, it's in our canon for all to read! Perhaps this private encounter speaks of the importance of passion in any relationship. Ethicist Paul Wadell notes:

Passion not only registers need, it also registers receptivity, for it suggests that whatever wholeness is lacking is brought to us through the agency of someone else. We are restored by someone other working on us, we are healed through an agency other than our own.[23]

The passion in Song of Songs understood in this light is a wonderful reminder that we need each other, and not just in an abstract way. Physical connection is vital. Babies left un-held will fail to thrive. Adults devoid of human contact will become isolated and self-destructive. But physical affection alone doesn't foster quality of life. Passion doesn't build the relationship in Song of Songs or in our lives. Rather, love of the other, made manifest in the physical relationship, is the foundation of relationship. We might call that romantic love.

The exuberance, the full-bodied-ness of Song of Songs, is an embrace of the affectivity that is uniquely and splendidly human, and a demonstration of the power of passion which seeks fulfillment. How else to describe love but through loving encounters? How else to understand the depth of God's desire for us? Thus, the early Jewish exegetes saw Song of Songs as a mystical reflection on God's love.

> Set me as a seal upon your heart, / as a seal upon your arm; / for love is strong as death, / passion fierce as the grave. / Its flashes are flashes of fire, / a raging flame. / Many waters cannot quench love, / neither can floods drown it. / If one offered for love / all the wealth of one's house, / it would be utterly scorned. (Song 8:6-7)

The culmination of friendship is a total giving of one's self to the other. Married couples know this experience, not only in their intimate encounters, but in the fidelity to the ordinariness of every day.

Song of Songs is an erotic, romantic pursuit and surrender of beloved and lover. Metaphorically, it has also been interpreted through the centuries as a description of the ultimate desire of God who longs to befriend us, and our passion for the God who seeks after us. The human experience of physical affectivity that springs from love is but a foretaste of what awaits the beloved of God. Wadell explains:

> In friendship with God we give ourself away, we surrender to the Spirit, and in that surrender our most exquisite individuality is secured, for we come to be what God in perfect love has always wanted us to be.[24]

Conclusion

All our friendships speak to us about what friendship with God can be like, but the intimate friendship between spouses most clearly presents the blessings and struggles of living as friends in the ordinariness of life. Indeed, Pat, whom I mentioned at the beginning of this chapter, was right. Marriage is so much more than going for ice cream! For those relationships that begin as friendship, the couple builds their lives on a solid foundation. But not all marriages begin among friends who have long known each other. My mother tells the story of her early courtship with my father who was in the Navy and stationed out of state. He had met both my mother and her sister on a home visit and began corresponding with the woman who would become my mother. But it was only upon a second home visit that he realized to which sister he had been writing! Like Abraham and Sarah, my mother left all she knew to travel "the Seven Seas," so to speak, with a man who would become her best friend for over fifty years.

As presented in our Scriptures, such marriages demonstrate duty, faithfulness, forgiveness, tenacity, and hope. In marriage, the friendship is transformed by presence, attraction, desire, and passion into a relationship of mutual self-giving. And at its most profound depths, such an intimate friendship reflects God's desire for us.

For Reflection:

- If you are married, were you friends with your spouse before your marriage or has your marriage brought you to friendship? If you are single, do you know couples whose marriage is based on a solid friendship? Did your parents share a true friendship?

- Reflect on your own experiences of affectivity in relationships. How have the physical encounters been made fuller by the quality of your relationship?

Chapter Four

When Good Friends Make Bad Mistakes: Recovery and Reconciliation

Introduction

"I wonder whatever happened to Vicki?" That pondering just a decade ago would have likely gone unanswered. Losing touch with high school friends or former work colleagues is par for the course in a modern, mobile society. But the advent of social media like Facebook suddenly provided a way to reconnect. After forty-five years, Vicki and I found each other virtually and discovered that we pretty much looked the same, minus the wrinkles and the gray hair! Facebook is the great aggregator of former and emerging relationships. But it doesn't do a good job of qualifying those relationships. In other words, not everyone you "friend" on your Facebook page fits the definition of "friend" as we've been describing it. While some folks may, indeed, have done good for you, or shared a mutual relationship, or helped you reach your potential, few fit the full definition. It's no surprise that the philosopher who spent much time describing the quality of friendship would also have insights on the different types of friends, as we noted in chapter 1. In Book 8 of his *Nichomachean Ethics*, Aristotle notes that there are

- friendships of utility;

- friendships of pleasure;

- friendships of the good.

Friendships of utility describes people with whom we are on cordial terms because it's mutually beneficial. Business associates, co-workers, and parents whose children play sports together are examples of this type of friendship. As Aristotle describes it, these relationships are transitory. When the need no longer exists, the friendship dissipates. For example, your kid no longer plays soccer so you don't connect with the soccer moms in the same way anymore. Since the relationship is based on fulfilling a mutual need, when the need is met these friendships often fade away. Jesus tells a parable about one such friend.

> Suppose one of you has a friend, and you go to him at midnight and say to him, "Friend, lend me three loaves of bread; for a friend of mine has arrived, and I have nothing to set before him." And he answers from within, "Do not bother me; the door has already been locked, and my children are with me in bed; I cannot get up and give you anything." I tell you, even though he will not get up and give him anything because he is his friend, at least because of his persistence he will get up and give him whatever he needs. (Luke 11:5-8)

We might consider some of those who encountered Jesus as these types of casual friends. Tax collectors, sinners, and beggars are welcomed by Jesus, so his detractors accuse him of being "a glutton and a drunkard, a friend of tax collectors and sinners" (Matthew 11:19, Luke 7:34). But only a very few of these become disciples. Matthew (Matthew 9:9), Mary of Magdala (Luke 8:1-3), and Bartimaeus (Mark 10:46-52) come to mind.

Friendships of pleasure describe those relationships that arise because of mutual joy or attraction. My sister meets weekly for a neighborhood game night. Those who gather around the table may not see each other the rest of the week or even care to develop a deeper friendship. They simply enjoy playing games and the companionship of others who share the same interest. To the extreme, friendships of pleasure describe those mutual casual sexual encounters in which neither person intends a long-term commitment. Like friendships of utility, these friendships are based on a single purpose, so when it is no longer fun or attractive or pleasurable, the relationships tend to end, and sometimes with tragic results. The death of John the Baptist illustrates an extreme result of this type of relationship. John had criticized Herod for marrying his brother's ex-wife.

Herod on his birthday gave a banquet for his courtiers and officers and for the leaders of Galilee. When his daughter Herodias came in and danced, she pleased Herod and his guests;

and the king said to the girl, "Ask me for whatever you wish, and I will give it." And he solemnly swore to her, "Whatever you ask me, I will give you, even half of my kingdom." (Mark 6:21-23)

The girl's mother held a grudge against John for criticizing her relationship with Herod, so she instructed her daughter to ask for John's head. Though Herod was sorry, he didn't want to break his oath before his guests. Immediately he sent a soldier to behead John the Baptist (Mark 6:27).

When Jesus learns of John's death, he withdraws to a lonely place apart (Matthew 14:13), suggesting he needed time and space to grieve and to pray (Mark 1:35, Luke 5:16). Jesus' response to the death of John witnesses to Aristotle's third and most prized category: friendships of the good. We long to be with these friends. To not only hear about their blessings and their struggles, but to be with them in those times; to mourn their loss.

These are friends upon whom we can depend. The centurion of Capernaum and Paul's friends are prime examples. Stricken over the illness of his servant, the centurion of Capernaum first sends a delegation of Jewish leaders to implore Jesus' help. But as Jesus nears, he sends his friends who say on his behalf, "Lord do not trouble yourself, for I am not worthy to have you come under my roof; therefore I did not presume to come to you. But only speak the word, and let my servant be healed" (Luke 7:6-7). During his numerous imprisonments, the apostle Paul thanks his friends for their support (Acts 24:23, 27:3) and for sharing in his troubles (Philippians 4:14-16). These friends are the people who make our lives rich by their friendship. And consequently, when these relationships are tested, bent, and sometimes broken beyond repair, the loss of these friendships are the ones we grieve the most.

Many passages of Scriptures recognize the pain suffered when a friend fails us:

It is not enemies who taunt me— / I could bear that; / it is not adversaries who deal insolently with me— / I could hide from them. / But it is you, my equal, / my companion, my familiar friend, / with whom I kept pleasant company; / we walked in the house of God with the throng. (Psalm 55:12-14)

But as Proverbs recognizes, not all friends are untrustworthy: "Some friends play at friendship / but a true friend sticks closer than one's nearest kin" (Proverbs 18:24). And to keep your friends sometimes you have to take the high road: "One who forgives an affront fosters friendship, / but one who dwells on disputes will alienate a friend" (17:9). Perhaps Sirach offers the best hope for repairing broken friendships:

One who throws a stone at birds scares them away, / and one who reviles a friend destroys a friendship. / Even if you draw your sword against a friend, / do not despair, for there is a way back.

/ If you open your mouth against your friend,
/ do not worry, for reconciliation is possible.
(22:20-22)

Sirach's admonition recognizes that relationships are hard, and on occasion we are not our best selves with our friends. Sometimes those friendships can be repaired, and sometimes, the friendship is dissolved. In what follows, we see examples of both.

A Road Diverged

In high school, Sue and I were inseparable. Same classes, same extracurricular activities. And then came college. My academic interests and hers weren't the same. She wanted to major in business. I would become a journalist. After four years of high school, a single semester of college drove us down different roads. We began to travel in new circles, make new friends, and see less and less of each other. In the throes of high school, we couldn't have imagined that our own professional and personal goals would separate us. But our proverbial roads diverged. The friendship didn't end so much as simply fade away.

I think of that faded high school friendship whenever I read the story of Barnabas and Paul in Acts of the Apostles. Our first encounters with Saul, who is also known as Paul, are not promising. He stands by while rabble-rousers stone Stephen (Acts 7:58), and later travels to Damascus intent on apprehending any men or women who believe in Jesus (9:1-2).

Soon after his dramatic encounter with the Lord on the road to Damascus, he travels back to Jerusalem. But no one trusts Paul's newfound faith until Barnabas takes charge of him and brings him to the apostles (9:27). Barnabas is described as a good man, full of both the Holy Spirit and faith (11:24). Later, he will travel to Tarsus to find Saul and invite him to join the missionary effort among the Gentiles in Antioch (11:25). After their work is completed, they return to Jerusalem now joined by John Mark, a cousin of Barnabas (12:25; see also Colossians 4:10).

> While they were worshiping the Lord and fasting, the Holy Spirit said, "Set apart for me Barnabas and Saul for the work to which I have called them." Then after fasting and praying they laid their hands on them and sent them off. (Acts 13:2-3)

Thus begins what will be known as Paul's First Missionary Journey. Barnabas, Saul, and their assistant, John Mark, sail from the port of Antioch in Syria to the island of Cyprus. During their mission on Cyprus, we learn that Saul is also called Paul (Acts 13:9). From there they sail to Perga on the coast of Asia Minor, where John Mark leaves the team and returns to Jerusalem (13:13). Barnabas and Paul make the arduous trip into the Pisidian mountains, evangelizing in Antioch of Pisidia, Iconium, Lystra, and Derbe (chapters 13–14). Retracing their steps, they return to Perga, make a stop at Attalia, and then sail to Antioch in Syria.

We can only imagine the hardships both face as they traverse the difficult terrain, encountering inhospitable locals and potential believers. When Paul plans a return visit, Barnabas wishes to take John Mark with them.

> But Paul decided not to take with them one who had deserted them in Pamphylia and had not accompanied them in the work. The disagreement became so sharp that they parted company; Barnabas took Mark with him and sailed away to Cyprus. (Acts 15:38-39)

As Acts presents it, the single most successful missionary team breaks up over a disagreement. After the years of arduous preaching and proselytizing, harrowing encounters and dangerous travels, Barnabas and Paul dissolve the band, so to speak. Paul will choose another travel companion, Silas, and the biblical story of Barnabas comes to an end (Acts 15:40). Barnabas, whose very name means encouragement, never failed to be a compassionate companion, giving John Mark a second chance as he had given Paul. He had taken Paul under his wing and helped him become a preacher. But as time went on, the two who were partners developed a disagreement that dissolved the partnership. In this case, the friends did not take Sirach's advice, and there was no reconciliation.

The Imperfect Friend

Sometimes a friendship just ends, and both must go their own way. But there are some situations when Sirach is affirmed, and reconciliation is possible. In the Gospel of John, we witness one of those second chances.

It all begins before Passover. Jesus knows his hour to depart this world has come, and "having loved his own who were in the world, he loved them to the end" (John 13:1). The story begins by announcing Jesus' love for his disciples to the "end." The Greek word is *telos*. When the word *telos* is used in Matthew 5:48 it is translated as "be perfect," and in 1 Corinthians 14:20 the same word is translated as "be mature." So, Jesus loves his disciples completely and perfectly, which is amazing given what two disciples of his inner circle will do.

In the first scene, we learn that the devil had already "put it into the heart of Judas" to betray Jesus (John 13:2). Jesus then proceeds to wash the disciples' feet even though "he knew who was to betray him" (13:11). Judas' impending betrayal brackets Peter's impetuous response to having his feet washed by his Master.

> "Lord, are you going to wash my feet?" Jesus answered, "You do not know now what I am doing, but later you will understand." Peter said to him, "You will never wash my feet." Jesus answered, "Unless I wash you, you have no share with me." Simon Peter said to him, "Lord, not my feet only but also my hands and my head!"

Jesus said to him, "One who has bathed does not need to wash, except for the feet, but is entirely clean. And you are clean, though not all of you." (13:6-10)

We get Peter's discomfort. We shake hands; we don't touch each other's feet. It seems overly personal. And the feet of first century folks, those who wear sandals and trudge up and down dusty hills, those feet must have been quite a sight. Sure, a sign of hospitality was to have one's feet cleansed before a banquet, but that dirty job was left to the household servants. Certainly, the one hosting the meal did not strip off his garments and assume the position of a slave. Peter isn't objecting to having his feet washed. He's objecting that Jesus is the one who's doing it. And as with the other disciples, Jesus washes the feet of Judas.

After he had washed their feet, had put on his robe, and had returned to the table, he said to them, "Do you know what I have done to you? You call me Teacher and Lord—and you are right, for that is what I am. So if I, your Lord and Teacher, have washed your feet, you also ought to wash one another's feet. For I have set you an example, that you also should do as I have done to you. Very truly, I tell you, servants are not greater than their master, nor are messengers greater than the one who sent them. If you know these things, you are blessed if you do them. (13:12-17)

This intimate act of kneeling before the other, cleaning the dirt of the day off their tired feet, refreshing them in body and also in spirit—this is the act of love of one friend toward another. Blessed are the disciples if they follow this example. But then Jesus adds: "I am not speaking of all of you; I know whom I have chosen. But it is to fulfill the scripture, 'The one who ate my bread has lifted his heel against me'" (John 13:18).

Jesus cites Psalm 41, the very verse that speaks of the betrayal of one's dear friend: "Even my bosom friend in whom I trusted, / who ate of my bread, has lifted the heel against me" (Psalm 41:9). Though Jesus will speak of his disciples as friends later in John's Gospel, here his citation of Psalm 41 indicates that Jesus has always seen them as more than mere followers. He will even call them his gift from God (John 17:6).

Jesus is deeply troubled and announces that one among the disciples will betray him. We can imagine the searching glances as the disciples scan the room. Who could it be? The moment Jesus hands a morsel of bread to Judas, Satan enters into the disciple. We could imagine that sadness and resignation with which Jesus now speaks: "Do quickly what you are going to do" (John 13:27). Judas goes to betray his *friend*.

In response to Judas' departure, Jesus announces that his glorification has begun. As the evangelist John understands the story, Judas' betrayal was a necessary act to initiate Jesus' glorification. On the heels of Judas' departure,

Jesus then gives his disciples a new commandment: love one another (John 13:34). The confirmation that someone is truly a disciple of Jesus is their love for their fellow disciples. This crowning moment is then dashed when Jesus pronounces that another one of his friends—Simon Peter—will disappoint. "Very truly, I tell you, before the cock crows, you will have denied me three times" (13:38).

In John chapter 13, the actions of Jesus, Judas, and Peter are interpreted through the lens of love and friendship. In verses 12-15 and 31-35 Jesus speaks of his actions as gift. That gift is framed by descriptions of two of his own who receive the gifts: Peter who will deny Jesus and Judas who will betray him. Our passage opens with an acknowledgement that despite the imperfection of his most intimate friends, Jesus, nonetheless, loves them perfectly.

The denial of Peter predicted by Jesus then occurs in John chapter 18, when three times Peter defends himself and so denies being a disciple of Jesus. Throughout the Gospel of John, Peter is presented as one possessing true potential. When he is brought to Jesus by his brother Andrew, Jesus immediately nicknames him "Cephas," or Peter, which means "rock" (John 1:40-44). When many disciples become disenchanted with Jesus and confused by his preaching on the bread of life, Jesus asks if the Twelve, too, would leave him. Peter answers simply, "Lord, to whom can we go? You have the words of eternal life" (6:68). After the foot-washing, Peter announces that he would lay down his life for Jesus (13:37). We can only imagine how disappointed Jesus must have been when the rock on which he depended had failed him when he needed him the most.

I continue to be astounded by the story of Judas, Peter, and Jesus, by the machinations of evil, the susceptibility of even trusted confidants, and Jesus' witness of love and service. But evil doesn't have the last word. It is within our friendships that we come to be better than we are. We see in our friend the friend we long to be, and that calls us toward growth.

Now we recall the refrain from Sirach "If you open your mouth against your friend, / do not worry, for reconciliation is possible" (Sirach 22:22). The relationship between Peter and Jesus does not end with denial or even death. In John chapter 21, Peter and the resurrected Jesus meet again on the shores of the sea. After having eaten together, Jesus turns to Peter and asks him three times if he loves him. We often see this scene as a parallel to the three times Peter denied Jesus. But what may escape our notice is the vocabulary that Jesus uses, only evident in the Greek. To appreciate Jesus' words, we need to know that Greek has three different terms for our one word "love." *Eros* refers to erotic love and the deep appreciation for beauty. *Philia* is the affection, esteem, and goodwill we experience toward our friends. Think of Philadelphia, the city of brotherly love. Finally, *agapē* is the love that God has for us, and we in turn should have for God. As Jesus notes, *agapē* is love that sacrifices itself for the other (John 15:13). *Agapē* was so foundational to early Christianity that the meals held within the community were known as "agapeic" to emphasis the fellowship among the believers.

When Jesus asks Peter if he loves him the first time, Jesus uses the verb, *agapas.*

"Peter, do you *agapas* me more than these?

Peter responds, "Yes, Lord; you know that I *philō* you."

By using the term *agapas,* Jesus is asking of Peter that type of love that lays down one's life for one's friend, the type of love that God has for us, an expansive, self-sacrificing love. Peter responds that he holds a friendship love—one based on doing good, reciprocating, and working toward the betterment of the friend.

Again Jesus asks Peter, "Do you *agapas* me?"

Peter doesn't hear the distinction. He responds, "You know that I *philō* you."

The third time Jesus asks, "Peter, do you *phileis* me?" And Peter responds, "You know that I *philō* you." One way to interpret this is as Jesus accepting Peter's weakness, his not being ready for the deepest kind of friendship and love being offered, and therefore changing his vocabulary. Peter is simply not yet ready to love as Jesus desires. Nonetheless, Jesus entrusts him with the care of the community, recognizing that friendship love leads to the kind of love that God asks of all God's children: *agapē.* Jesus' prophetic statement of what awaits Peter indicates that when required Peter will sacrifice everything to glorify God (John 21:18-19). His *philia* will become *agapē.*

Reconciliation

Reconciliation is not forgetting. Reconciliation isn't only forgiving. Reconciliation means meeting friends were they are—in their imperfection—and loving them anyway. The process of reconciliation is modeled by Jesus, who not only reconciles with the very disciple who denied him, but then commissions him, "Tend my sheep." Simon Peter is transformed into a true disciple and sent out on mission, on the way he will show concretely his "friendship" with Jesus.

But what of Judas? He had been one of the chosen Twelve (Mark 3:19). He had been responsible for the group's finances (John 13:29). And even at the Garden of Gethsemane, Jesus called Judas "friend" (Matthew 26:50). Does Jesus mean this ironically having been betrayed by a kiss from Judas? Perhaps. But at the Last Supper in the Gospel of John, Jesus clearly knows of Judas' impending betrayal. It is Satan who enters Judas and therefore Satan who is responsible for the evil machinations (John 13:27). After the betrayal, we hear nothing more in the Gospel of John. But the evangelist Matthew includes a story about his fate:

> When Judas, his betrayer, saw that Jesus was condemned, he repented and brought back the thirty pieces of silver to the chief priests and the elders. He said, "I have sinned by betraying innocent blood." But they said, "What is that to us? See to it yourself." Throwing down the pieces of silver in

the temple, he departed; and he went and hanged himself. (Matthew 27:3-5; cf. an alternate version in Acts 1:16-20)

Throughout history, the word "Judas" has become synonymous with the friend who betrays. But some early Church Fathers recognized that his action of betrayal led to the Passion and subsequent resurrection of Jesus. In his commentary on Matthew, the third-century Church Father Origen of Alexandria argued that Judas did repent of his sins, but he failed to receive reconciliation because he made himself judge and jury by committing suicide.[25]

In the 1970s, a second-century gnostic (heretical) gospel was discovered known as "The Gospel of Judas." Judas is presented as possessing keen insight that surpasses the other disciples. Jesus speaks to Judas privately:

Step away from the others and I shall tell you the mysteries of the kingdom. It is possible for you to reach it, but you will grieve a great deal (35).[26]

But beyond these snippets, the fate of Judas has been left to our imagination. One of the most poignant reflections is the poem "The Judas Tree" by D. Ruth Etchells.[27] It imagines the reconciliation between Jesus and the disciple who betrayed him.

In Hell there grew a Judas Tree
Where Judas hanged and died
Because he could not bear to see

His master crucified
Our Lord descended into Hell
And found his Judas there
For ever hanging on the tree
Grown from his own despair
So Jesus cut his Judas down
And took him in his arms
"It was for this I came" he said
"And not to do you harm
My Father gave me twelve good men
And all of them I kept
Though one betrayed and one denied
Some fled and others slept
In three days' time I must return
To make the others glad
But first I had to come to Hell
And share the death you had
My tree will grow in place of yours
Its roots lie here as well
There is no final victory
Without this soul from Hell"
So when we all condemned him
As of every traitor worst
Remember that of all his men
Our Lord forgave him first.

Conclusion

We may not have betrayed or denied our friends as did
Judas and Peter, but likely there have been moments in our

friendships when we have not responded well. Or perhaps, we were the ones our friends disappointed or abandoned. We are reminded by our Scriptures that that experience of pain and loss is not the final story. As Proverbs advises: "One who forgives an affront fosters friendship" (Proverbs 17:9). And Jesus has shown us the way by his reconciliation with the disciple who denied him: "Feed my sheep."

For Reflection:

- No doubt we have all had experiences of friends who failed us. Who comes to mind as you ponder those broken friendships? Was reconciliation ever possible?

- Imagine the setting of the Last Supper and picture yourself as Judas or Peter. Then read John chapter 21. Imagine Jesus inviting you to a deeper, more perfect friendship. How might you extend that reconciliation to your former friends?

Chapter Five

Befriending Myself:
Moving beyond Personal Limitations

Introduction

The first semester away at college is often a crisis moment for many young adults. As a campus minister at a Catholic university, my job was to help eighteen-year-olds balance their new freedom with a sense of personal responsibility and moral integrity. Most often the foundation laid by their parents and grandparents was enough to steer them away from mistakes they would later regret. But not always.

Several times throughout the fall, I had run into Susan. She was making the most of the various social activities but seemed a little less enthusiastic about academic pursuits. As the semester progressed, I saw less of her at university ministry activities, until finally she stopped attending Sunday liturgy. My texts and phone messages went unanswered. Toward the end of the semester, to my surprise she appeared at my office door and burst into tears.

The sexual experimentation, the drinking, and the partying had seduced her, and she felt a wave of remorse and guilt that she had traveled so far beyond her moral compass.

"I don't want to be this person," she sobbed. "I don't like me. I don't like anything about me. Can I start over?"

"Always," was my answer. "Always." We are made a little less than angels, so Psalm 8:5 reminds us. The prophets announce we are the apple of God's eye (Zechariah 2:8) and loved by God with an everlasting love (Jeremiah 31:3). God begs us to return to our God (Hosea 14:1-4) who is ever forgiving (Isaiah 43:25-26).

In our pursuit of friendship with God, we have explored our relationships with spouses, our children, and our imperfect friends, but the single most important person with whom we are to be friends is ourselves. Without that primary experience, we can hardly be friends with others. How can we truly receive the love of another, or experience forgiveness and reconciliation, if we are estranged from ourselves? Susan had come to realize that she had lost sight of her own value, had been overwhelmed by the new social and academic demands, and was beating herself up for her mistakes. "Can I get a mulligan (in golf, an extra stroke after a bad shot)?" we ask God. And as the Bible demonstrates, the answer is "Always."

From Murderer to Friend of God

We are familiar with the story of Moses leading the Hebrews out of slavery in Egypt and their subsequent forty-year sojourn in the desert. But Israel's greatest prophet had ignominious beginnings. As the story is told in Exodus chapters 1 and 2, the Hebrews had grown numerous and the Egyptian pharaoh worried about a revolt. He ordered that the Hebrew baby boys be thrown into the river (Exodus 1:22). Moses' mother hides her infant son as long as she can, but eventually, she places him in a watertight basket and sends him adrift on the river (2:3-4). If we read the story carefully, we see the ingenuity of the mother of Moses. In essence, she did abide by Pharaoh's command. But she strategically sets the basket into the water near where Pharaoh's daughter is bathing. Additionally, the sister of Moses stations herself on the bank to see what would happen. When Pharaoh's daughter discovers the child, the sister of Moses offers to find her a wet nurse and retrieves Moses' own mother (2:7-9). Mother and son are reunited, though in a new and different relationship.

From his narrow escape as a baby floating in a basket on the Nile, Moses grows up to be a significant member of Pharaoh's household. But Moses discovers that he is not a prince but a member of the Hebrew slave class. When he sees an Egyptian beating a fellow Hebrew, he kills the Egyptian and buries the body (Exodus 2:11-15).

In fear, Moses runs away to a very remote mountain desert of the Sinai Peninsula, becoming a shepherd with the tribal folks of Midian (Exodus 3:15). A difficult start, a privileged upbringing, a seriously bad deed, and fleeing the consequences—a pretty violent beginning for the future leader of the Israelites, one whom God will call God's intimate friend (33:17)!

But then it got even better.

Time passes and Moses begins a new life in Midian. While tending the flock of his father-in-law, Moses comes to Mount Horeb where he encounters a burning bush. Curiosity draws him to the unnatural sight. A voice calls out, addressing Moses by name! (Exodus 3:4). The voice commands Moses to remove his sandals, for he is now standing on holy ground. It would seem that Moses doesn't know the voice, for in the next moment, we hear, "'I am the God of your father, the God of Abraham, the God of Isaac, and the God of Jacob.' And Moses hid his face, for he was afraid to look at God" (3:6). God has witnessed the sufferings of the Hebrews, whom God calls "my people" (3:7), and now God will send Moses to act in God's stead to rescue his people (3:10). There is no recounting of Moses' murderous act. No expectation of repentance. No demand for justice. No punishment. It is not Moses' past deeds but his future mission that concerns God. It would seem that Moses gets a mulligan.

But while God may not address Moses' mistakes, Moses is well aware of his limitations. "Who am I that I should go to Pharaoh, and bring the Israelites out of Egypt?" (Exodus 3:11). "But suppose they do not believe me or listen to me" (4:1). "I am slow of speech and slow of tongue" (4:10). "O my Lord, please send someone else" (4:13). Throughout their subsequent relationship, Moses will complain and frequently ask God to relieve him of his responsibility (Exodus 5:22, 6:12, 33:12; Numbers 11:11) and the constant grumbling of the Israelites (Exodus 16:3).

But God's motion is forward, not backward. And, like Moses, though we may see ourselves as unworthy, without skill, and lacking in moral fortitude, God knows otherwise.

Most of us, thank God, have not found ourselves in the shoes of young Moses, standing over the body of the Egyptian whom he had killed. However, many of us have engaged in activities that have harmed ourselves or others. But that wasn't the end of our story.

Set into the hillside in upstate New York, New Hope Manor is a testament to the tenacity of the human spirit. A residential substance abuse center for young women established in 1970, New Hope grew out of the work of Fr. Daniel Egan, SA, the "junkie priest," who recognized the dignity of each person. He noted,

> If we had the vision of faith, we would see beneath every behavior—no matter how repulsive—beneath every bodily appearance—no matter how dirty or deformed—a priceless dignity and value that makes all material facts and scientific technologies fade into insignificance.[28]

But as a counselor at New Hope and later director, Sr. Maureen Conway, O.P., recognized that the difficulty is not for the ministers and counselors to see the innate dignity of those suffering from addiction, but for the woman herself to come to know that she is worthy, beloved of God, and forgiven. The first step of recovery is to believe you are worth the effort.

Moses could only see his limitations, but God had a wider vision. As Paul Wadell writes, "God sees our fullest potential—our redeemed and holy self—and God loves us in a way that beckons this self to life."[29]

Fulfilling Potential

But we don't see as God sees, so it's sometimes hard to trust that we are indeed on the right track. Thomas Merton captured this hesitancy in his prayer:

> My Lord God, I have no idea where I am going. / I do not see the road ahead of me. / I cannot know for certain where it will end. / Nor do I really know myself, / and the fact that I think I am following Your will does not mean that I am actually doing so. / But I believe that the desire to please You does in fact please You.[30]

How do I reach my fullest potential? That was exactly the question with which Megan struggled.

She had a wonderful husband, a challenging job, friends and colleagues she admired. But there was one thing, that one missing piece that Megan longed for. She wanted to be a mother. One by one her college friends were becoming parents, delighting in the pregnancy, the birth, the feelings of overwhelming love and joy. How hard it was to share their joy while hiding her own sorrow. Six pregnancies all ended in miscarriage, and she deeply mourned her lost children. After every medical option was exhausted, Megan was left with only her abiding confidence that God was a God of life. And to this God, she poured out her heart, her feelings of inadequacy, her sense of failure as a woman.

Like a thread woven throughout our Scriptures, the numerous stories of barren women echo Megan's lament. Sarai who would become Sarah is barren despite God's promise of progeny (Genesis 11:30). Isaac's wife, Rebekah, is unable to bear children (25:21), and Rachel, the beloved wife of Jacob, will suffer similarly (29:31). The nameless mother of Samson had been barren until an appearance by an angel (Judges 13:3). Psalm 113:9 speaks of a barren woman whom God blesses. The Book of Isaiah echoes the psalm, announcing, "Sing, O barren one who did not bear; / burst into song and shout, / you who have not been in labor! / For the children of the desolate woman will be more / than the children of her that is married, says the LORD" (54:1). And in the New Testament we hear of Elizabeth who had no children because of her advancing age (Luke 1:7). Perhaps the most poignant narrative, one in which we actually hear the voice of the distraught woman, is the story of Hannah in 1 Samuel chapters 1–2.

The story begins with a man, Elkanah, who has two wives, Hannah whom he loves dearly but is childless, and Peninnah, who has borne children (1 Samuel 1:1-5). Year after year when the family makes a pilgrimage to Shiloh, Peninnah antagonizes and reproaches Hannah for her barrenness. In response, Hannah becomes depressed, weeping and refusing to eat. Her pleading husband's words echo the efforts of many husbands who try to understand their wives' struggle. "Hannah, why do you weep? Why do you not eat? Why is your heart sad? Am I not more to you than ten sons?" (1:8).

Hannah rises from the table and goes to the tent of the Lord to pour out her sorrow and misery. In the ancient context, a married woman was to produce heirs for her husband, and failure to bear children meant a woman had been cursed (Genesis 30:1-2). When a woman was widowed, she became the responsibility of her son (Leviticus 19:3). A woman without children had to hope that other family members would come to her aid (Ruth 1:1,19). A barren woman not only bore the shame of having been forgotten by God, but she was also in a precarious social situation. Hannah has great reason to cry out to God and lament her situation.

She begs God for a son, promising to dedicate him to God. In our twenty-first century context, Hannah's prayer seems a bit confusing. She desperately wants a son yet is willing to give him back to God, in essence to spend his life in service to the cult center at Shiloh. Her prayers are so heartfelt and demonstrative that the local priest, Eli, thinks she is intoxicated! "How long will you make a drunken spectacle of yourself? Put away your wine" (1 Samuel 1:14).

Poor Hannah replies, "No, my lord, I am a woman deeply troubled; I have drunk neither wine nor strong drink, but I have been pouring out my soul before the

LORD. Do not regard your servant as a worthless woman, for I have been speaking out of my great anxiety and vexation all this time" (1 Samuel 1:15-16).

Eli recovers from his misjudgment and sends Hannah away in peace, promising that God will grant her petition. Indeed, later Hannah conceives and gives birth to a son whom she names Samuel. After he is weaned, Hannah has the child presented to the elderly priest, saying that he has been dedicated to God (1 Samuel 1:25-28). She entrusts Eli with her most valuable possession. Hannah has her prayers answered. She has fulfilled her society's expectation, and she sings a song of joy:

My heart exults in the LORD; / my strength is exalted in my God. / My mouth derides my enemies, / because I rejoice in my victory. / There is no Holy One like the LORD, / no one besides you; / there is no Rock like our God. / Talk no more so very proudly, / let not arrogance come from your mouth; / for the LORD is a God of knowledge, / and by him actions are weighed. / The bows of the mighty are broken, / but the feeble gird on strength. / Those who were full have hired themselves out for bread, / but those who were hungry are fat with spoil. / The barren has borne seven, / but she who has many children is forlorn. / The LORD kills and brings to life; / he brings down to Sheol and raises up. / The LORD makes poor and makes rich; / he brings low, he also exalts. / He raises up the poor from the dust; / he lifts the needy from the ash heap, / to make them sit with princes / and inherit a seat of honor. / For the pillars of the earth are the LORD's, / and on them he has set the world. (2:1-8)

Hannah's canticle will become the template for Mary in her own song of joy in Luke 1:47-55, which begins with the resounding proclamation: "My soul magnifies the Lord, / and my spirit rejoices in God my Savior, / for he has looked with favor on the lowliness of his servant" (verses 46-48).

We all—men and women—are hard-wired for life, the producing, nurturing, and protecting of life. When circumstances prevent us from pursuing our creativity, or expressing our generativity, we can fall prey to self-doubt and, in some cases, self-loathing. Hannah becomes a model for us. She brought her deep sadness to God, trusting that God would hear and respond. But God doesn't always respond as we hoped or in a timely manner. Megan continues to grieve the six babies she lost. Throughout the journey she has felt doubt, rage, and abandonment. And while she will always feel the sense of her incomplete family, today Megan sings the same song of joy as Hannah. Her two beautiful and lively children are a testament to her tenacity of faith and abiding trust that "nothing will be impossible with God" (Luke 1:37).

A New Vocation

The story of the persecutor Saul becoming the apostle Paul is a textbook example that "nothing will be impossible with God." So important is his story of reorientation that the author of Acts of the Apostles tells it three times: Acts 9:1-19, 22:3-21, and 26:9-20. But for our purposes, let's see what Paul says about the experience himself. In his Letter to the Galatians, Paul writes, "you have heard, no doubt, of my earlier life in Judaism. I was violently persecuting the church of God and was trying to destroy it" (Galatians 1:13). Though he claims to be an apostle, Paul admits, "For I am the least of the apostles, unfit to be called an apostle, because I persecuted the church of God" (1 Corinthians 15:9). Paul readily acknowledges his role in attacking the early followers of Christ: "as to zeal, a persecutor of the church; as to righteousness under the law, blameless. Yet whatever gains I had, these I have come to regard as loss because of Christ. More than that, I regard everything as loss because of the surpassing value of knowing Christ Jesus my Lord" (Philippians 3:6-8). How did that happen? What turned Paul around? Nothing short of the mercy of God.

In his Second Letter to the Corinthians, Paul acknowledges that he has his ministry by the mercy of God (2 Corinthians 4:1). He has renounced disgraceful, underhanded ways (4:2), likely alluding to his past actions against the church. Having been "mercied" by God, Paul experiences the glory of Christ (4:4) and "the glory of God in the face of Jesus Christ" (4:6), perhaps referencing his revelatory encounter with Jesus Christ (Galatians 1:16, Acts 9:3-5). Paul announces that the most amazing thing has happened. He got a do-over!

> For the love of Christ urges us on, because we are convinced that one has died for all; therefore all have died. And he died for all, so that those who live might live no longer for themselves, but for him who died and was raised for them. From now on, therefore, we regard no one from a human point of view; even though we once knew Christ from a human point of view, we know him no longer in that way. So if anyone is in Christ, there is a new creation: everything old has passed away; see, everything has become new! (2 Corinthians 5:14-17)

In the Greco-Roman context, the one who offended or broke the relationship had the responsibility of initiating the restoration of the relationship and of ending the enmity. Paul radically upsets the paradigm, changing the direction of reconciliation. God, as the offended party, initiates the reconciliation, "not counting their trespasses against them" (2 Corinthians 5:19), even though humanity continued in sin (Romans 5:8) and remained hostile to God (Romans 5:10). The death of Christ is a reparation within the standard paradigm, but it is God who makes the reparation here (Romans 5:10, 2 Corinthians 5:18-19). Paul comes to understand that not only did God forgive his sin, but God through Christ has forgiven all. Paul is now invited to a new vocation.

All this is from God, who reconciled us to himself through Christ, and has given us the ministry of reconciliation; that is, in Christ God was reconciling the world to himself, not counting their trespasses against them, and entrusting the message of reconciliation to us. So we are ambassadors for Christ, since God is making his appeal through us; we entreat you on behalf of Christ, be reconciled to God. For our sake he made him to be sin who knew no sin, so that in him we might become the righteousness of God. (2 Corinthians 5:18-21)

Without reparations or punishment, Paul, the former persecutor, was reconciled by God's grace through Christ's death. The same opportunity given to Paul is given to us. But as Paul recognizes, once reconciled with God, we are now called to be ambassadors of that good news of reconciliation to others. Indeed, a mulligan awaits us all!

Conclusion

Moses, Hannah, and Paul offer biblical examples of individuals who have felt unworthy either due to their own mistakes or to the hand that fate dealt them. Moses couldn't imagine that God would call him, a fugitive from justice, to be leader of God's people. Hannah felt forsaken, despite the love of her husband. Paul openly persecuted the church of God. Their individual encounters with

God enabled them to move beyond their limitations and personal pain. Moses becomes Israel's greatest prophet, an intimate friend of God (Exodus 33:12). Hannah's son, Samuel, becomes the prophet who will anoint David king (1 Samuel 16:13). Paul becomes the Apostle to the Gentiles (Romans 1:1-6, 11:13; Acts 9:15). Through their encounters with God, Moses, Hannah, and Paul came to realize their true potential. Something a woman named Marie knows much about.

Marie is enthusiastic about her recovery. This day she has been drug-free for ten months, perhaps the greatest milestone in her life. When asked how she has survived the first few difficult months and emerged so peaceful, she responds, "God has been with me. I couldn't have done it without God. I just can't say enough about him."

She continues, bubbling with a rush of new life, "I'm having an open house on Saturday." She had been homeless during much of her drug addiction and early recovery. Most recently, she lived at a Catholic shelter in Chicago. "An open house with lots of food. Chicken and greens. And cake . . . can you come?" She is like a child at Christmas, enamored by the possibilities in all the packages.

With a two-year-old now in her custody, she looks to the future. A twenty-six-year-old woman announcing to all who will hear that "God has saved me." Inviting any who would come to celebrate that saving act with a festival. A recovering drug addict and once-homeless woman now proclaiming a gospel of good news rooted in her own experience of God's saving action. When we befriend ourselves, we free ourselves to befriend the world.

For Reflection

- Are there things that you've done in the past that prevent you from moving forward? Consider asking God for a "mulligan," a "do-over," so that you might move more freely into the future.

- How have you experienced generativity at different stages in your life? Have you experienced "barrenness" and felt the deep sadness of Hannah? With whom have you been able to share your sorrow?

Chapter Six

What a Friend We Have in Jesus: Becoming Friends of God

Introduction

I prefer maps, something I can hold in my hand. I can see where I've come from and chart for myself where I want to go and how to get there. So, when a sister in my religious congregation received a GPS as a gift, I was none too thrilled. The disembodied computer-generated voice blandly directed me left or right. When I chose a different direction, she would announce, "Recalculating." I didn't want to be "recalculated." I wanted to go my way. If only Ms. GPS had been a person, then I could have explained this. Being face to face is a much better way of communicating. So I understand Moses' desire to speak to God face to face.

Moses had just dealt with the infidelity of the people who in his absence had built a golden calf (Exodus chapter 32). And now God announces that because of these "stiff-necked people," God will no longer travel with them (33:1-6). Moses intercedes again. At the end of his discourse, Moses asks the impossible: "Show me your glory" (33:18). Moses wants to see the face of God. Moses needs to see God, but to do so is to die (33:20). Instead God offers an alternative:

See, there is a place by me where you shall stand on the rock; and while my glory passes by I will put you in a cleft of the rock, and I will cover you with my hand until I have passed by; then I will take away my hand, and you shall see my back; but my face shall not be seen. (33:21-23)

The rabbis reflected on this passage metaphorically. They proposed that one cannot see God's actions in the present. One can only see where God has been in one's life. Seeing God face to face is always in hindsight.

As we have explored in previous chapters, through our friendships we have an experience of goodness, mutuality, and betterment that is analogous to God's love for us. Through our friends, we glimpse the glory of God. And though we may not recognize it in the moment, our friendships with others prepare us for friendship with God. Given that we cannot see God, it might seem outrageous, blasphemous, to presume we could be friends with but friendship with God has strong biblical roots.

...or Moments

In Genesis chapter 12, we meet a migrant, first known as Abram, formerly of Ur, an ancient city of the Sumerians. We have no indication as to why God chose Abram. We are only told that God directs Abram to leave his family and his home and to travel to a land that God will show him. As a result of Abram's blind obedience, God will make him a great nation, and he will be a blessing to all the earth. We may know this story, but we might miss the real kicker at the end: "Abram was seventy-five years old when he departed from Haran" (12:4).

God did not choose Abram because he was young and brimming with youthful energy. He was seventy-five years old! Nonetheless, Abram responds without hesitation to God's invitation. He takes everything and sets out for the land of Canaan. But as we learn, the journey is wrought with difficulties: famines, conflicts, blessings, and births. Twice the biblical author comments that the journey is accomplished incrementally: "And Abram journeyed on by stages toward the Negeb" (Genesis 12:9). "He journeyed on by stages from the Negeb as far as Bethel" (13:3). This incremental advance mirrors the developing relationship between Abraham and God:

- After these things the word of the LORD came to Abram in a vision, "Do not be afraid, Abram, I am your shield; your reward shall be very great." . . . And he believed the LORD; and the LORD reckoned it to him as righteousness. (15:1, 6)

- When Abram was ninety-nine years old, the LORD appeared to Abram, and said to him, "I am God Almighty; walk before me, and be blameless. And I will make my covenant between me and you, and will make you exceedingly numerous." (17:1-2)

- Some time afterward, God put Abraham to the test and said to him: Abraham! "Here I am!" he replied. (22:1, NABRE)

"After these things," "when Abram was ninety-nine years old," "some time afterward" . . . the encounter between God and Abram, which becomes the very foundation of Israel's and our own subsequent relationships with God, took time and testing. Abraham doesn't always cooperate with God's designs, like when he passes his wife off as his sister so as to save his own skin (Genesis 12:13). And even when he does appear to respond graciously (18:1-5), he doesn't simply bend to God's will. When the Lord reveals what will happen to Sodom and Gomorrah, Abraham offers a "what if" scenario.

Then Abraham came near and said, "Will you indeed sweep away the righteous with the wicked? Suppose there are fifty righteous within the city; will you then sweep away the place and not forgive it for the fifty righteous who are in it? Far be it from you to do such a thing, to slay the righteous with the wicked, so that the righteous fare as the wicked! Far be that from you! Shall not the Judge of all the earth do what is just?" (18:23-25)

This begins a back and forth between God and Abraham until finally, "[Abraham] said, 'Oh do not let the Lord be angry if I speak just once more. Suppose ten are found there.' He answered, 'For the sake of ten I will not destroy it'" (18:32). It would seem that true friends can challenge each other, remind them of their better natures, and redirect their efforts. And later biblical writers would recognize this relationship between Abraham and God as a friendship (2 Chronicles 20:7, Isaiah 411:8). Relationships of substance require time, tending, and patience, even relationships with God. Abraham came to know God through the many ups and downs of his living into the promise. "Thus the scripture was fulfilled that says, 'Abraham believed God, and it was reckoned to him as righteousness,' and he was called the friend of God" (James 2:23).

Encountering the Holy Stranger

Abraham and God's friendship developed over time, but there are moments when a chance encounter with a stranger brings us divine insights, though often only in hindsight.

In 1999, I was working on an archaeological dig in Israel. Catholic Theological Union, a school of theology and ministry in Chicago, was running a study trip to Syria, and I badly wanted to join them. But Israel and Syria have no diplomatic relations so in order to get to Damascus, I needed first to fly to Jordan before flying into Syria. A variety of bad happenstances occurred so that I missed my flight to Amman and the connecting one to Damascus. I wound up sleeping in the Tel Aviv airport, and catching the 6 a.m. flight to Amman the next day. Now my only mode of transport to Damascus at this point was a shared taxi from the city center of Amman. When I finally secured transport, I was loaded into a 1984 Impala along with five others. The men rode in the front seat. In the backseat were a young Muslim woman who spoke English and a very old Bedouin woman who did not, and me. About an hour and a half into the desert drive (did I mention there was no air conditioning?), the driver pulled over to get gas. Everyone hurried out of the vehicle. I stood there a bit perplexed. Seeing my confusion, the Bedouin woman took me by the hand and led me around the back … to the bathrooms!

Afterwards, I was rummaging around in my backpack for something to eat. I pulled out my jar of peanut butter (a staple for travelers!) and a spoon. The Bedouin woman pulled bread from her bag. We looked at each other and smiled. Her bread and my peanut butter made a wonderful "Eucharist" on the desert road to Damascus.

I thought often of that encounter, particularly after 9/11, when we immediately turned a defensive and suspicious eye on all Muslims. I remembered the kindly Bedouin. I learned from this elderly woman that welcoming the stranger as a friend can lead to profound eucharistic moments.

Though Abraham wouldn't have used those words to describe his encounter with a stranger, he seems to have a similar profound experience when he meets a Canaanite king who is a priest. The Melchizedek scene in Genesis 14:18-20 is inserted into an encounter with the king of Sodom (verses 17,21-24), within a chapter that doesn't fit with the surrounding narrative. In chapter 12, we were introduced to Abram (he won't become Abraham until chapter 17), and in chapter 15, God will make a magnificent covenant with Abram. But here in chapter 14, Abram is barely mentioned.

> And King Melchizedek of Salem brought out bread and wine; he was priest of God Most High. He blessed him and said, / "Blessed be Abram by God Most High, / maker of heaven and earth; / and blessed be God Most High, / who has delivered your enemies into your hand!" / And Abram gave him one-tenth of everything. (14:18-20)

Melchizedek is a Canaanite priest and king, whose name in Hebrew describes him. He is *melek* (king) of *zedek* (righteousness) from Salem, likely the Canaanite city that would become Jerusalem. In fact, Melchizedek is a priest of the "Most High God," an old Canaanite cult of *el elyon* (Most High God) practiced in ancient Jerusalem.

Abram is blessed by this stranger, and then offers him a tithe, thereby accepting the blessing. Far from disparaging the Canaanite priest and king, in verse 22 Abram unites his God, "the LORD," with the king's god. After he declines the king of Sodom's support, Abram announces, "I have sworn to the LORD, God Most High, maker of heaven and earth" (Genesis 14:22). The word we see in our Bibles as LORD is the holy name of God, Yahweh. Abram recognizes that Yahweh is the Most High God whom Melchizedek serves. In fact, here is the first time we hear of Yahweh being called the Most High God. From here out it will become commonplace and sometimes substitute for the holy name of God.

We don't have enough information to know if Melchizedek and Abram could be considered friends, though they do appear to mutually respect each other. What we do learn is that Abram's openness and hospitality to this Canaanite stranger gave him insights about his own understanding of God.

A Friend for the Long Haul

Sixteen hours of driving from Boston to Fort Lauderdale is enough to test any friendship. The first few hours sail by with conversation, music, more conversation, and stops for gasoline. But soon fatigue sets in. Questions arise: "Why didn't we fly?" "Where's the next rest area?" "Why is my bottom numb?" Eventually, conversation ceases, and each mile stretches on like a thousand. "Are we there yet?" isn't so much a question as a plea. A road warrior of many long drives, I can well understand the back and forth relation-ship between Moses and God. These two were on the road together for forty years!

Throughout the Pentateuch (the first five books of the Bible), we see countless interactions between Moses and God, beginning with their first meeting at the burning bush (Exodus chapter 3). As with that first encounter, there is a bit of back and forth. God proposes, Moses reacts, God reiterates, Moses responds. Sometimes it is Moses who is the voice of reason. After the incident with the golden calf, God announces:

> "Now let me alone, so that my wrath may burn hot against them and I may consume them; and of you I will make a great nation." But Moses implored the LORD his God, and said, "O LORD, why does your wrath burn hot against your people, whom you brought out of the land of Egypt with great power and with a mighty hand?" (32:10-11)

Moses and God speak regularly. In Exodus 33:11, we read "the LORD used to speak to Moses face to face, as one speaks to a friend." The verb form "used to speak" implies a "recurring pattern of behavior over the long term."[31] As we noted above, actually seeing God face to face would result in death. Here the narrator is emphasizing the personal nature of their conversation. And as we would expect in a friendship, the two don't always agree. God doesn't want to continue to travel with the Israelites because they "are a stiff-necked people" (33:5). Moses plays the friend card:

> Moses said to the LORD, "See, you have said to me, 'Bring up this people'; but you have not let me know whom you will send with me. Yet you have said, 'I know you by name, and you have also found favor in my sight.'" (33:12)

Moses bargains with God on the grounds of friendship, "Now if I have found favor . . ." (33:13), and God's mind is changed: "My presence will go with you" (33:14). But Moses isn't convinced, saying, "If your presence will not go . . ." (33:15). And God confirms God will be present on the journey because of their friendship: "The LORD said to Moses, 'I will do the very thing that you have asked; for you have found favor in my sight, and I know you by name.'" (33:17)

Other translations interpret "I know you by name" as "intimate friend," since in the context of the ancient Near East, only family and friends would know and use personal names. How far we have come from Moses and God's first encounter! At that time Moses had prematurely asked for God's name (3:13) before their relationship had even begun.

A God with Skin On

The oft-told story goes something like this. A little child awakes in the night as a furious thunderstorm roars outside. "Daddy, I'm scared!" the child cries out. The father, not wanting to get out of bed, calls back, "Don't worry. It's okay. God loves you and will take care of you." After a momentary pause, the child answers, "I know God loves me, but right now, I need somebody with skin on." I think most of us would agree. There are moments in our lives when we just need a God with skin on.

The Gospel of John gets this. "The Word became flesh and lived among us" (John 1:14). That God's creative activity became incarnate remains one of the more amazing tenets of Christian faith. As Karl Rahner, one of the great Catholic theologians of the twentieth century, wrote of the Incarnation, "God is the prodigal that squanders himself."[32] The Gospel of John will go on to describe the signs by which Jesus' true identity will be made known. But for the Word to be effective in its mission of salvation, it must first be enfleshed. Embodied. Jesus is our God with skin on.

Throughout the Gospel of John, Jesus tells his followers that he and the Father are one (John 10:30), everything that belongs to God also belongs to Jesus (16:15), and if his disciples believe in him, they, too, may be one with the Father and the Son (17:21). As Jesus nears his death, he gathers for one last meal. Around this table, Jesus invites his disciples into a new relationship.

This is my commandment, that you love one another as I have loved you. No one has greater love than this, to lay down one's life for one's friends. You are my friends if you do what I command you. I do not call you servants any longer, because the servant does not know what the master is doing; but I have called you friends, because I have made known to you everything that I have heard from my Father. You did not choose me but I chose you. And I appointed you to go and bear fruit, fruit that will last, so that the Father will give you whatever you ask him in my name.

I am giving you these commands so that you may love one another. (John 15:12-17)

Jesus is radically reorienting the relationship with his disciples. No longer is it between a master and a slave. Now it is a relationship between friend and friend. His disciples have become children of God. But this invitation to friendship is not only for the disciples; it extends to all who believe (20:29-31).

Being God's Friend Face to Face

Abraham is righteous before God, Moses is a servant and prophet of God, and Jesus is God's Son. As we have seen throughout our Scriptures, God is inviting human beings to friendship with the divine, a relationship that shares qualities with human friendships. The first quality of friendship with God is longevity, as exemplified by God's relationship with both Abraham and Moses. A dramatic moment (invitation to leave everything, voice in a burning bush) may initiate the relationship, but that isn't what sustains it. Think of all the other dramatic divine encounters depicted in our Scriptures. Few of them result in friendship with God. As with our human friendships, the test of time, turmoil, and transition either make or break our relationships. Becoming friends with God is a lifelong commitment.

Another somewhat surprising quality of divine friendship is its personal nature. God knows our name. And we know God's. Jesus tells his disciples that he and the Father are one, so "Whoever has seen me has seen the Father" (John 14:9). Friendship with Jesus leads us to friendship with God, since shared friendship is in God's very nature. Think of the Trinity. And that personal, intimate relationship is based on trust. We're confident that we, like Abraham and Moses, can disagree with God. There is a give and take in friendship that comes from confidence and trust.

But friendship is not without costs. In John 15:12, Jesus gives the disciples one command—that they love one another as he has loved them. Jesus doesn't use the standard Greek word for friendship love (*philia*). He uses *agapē*. The type of love that Jesus demands requires the willingness to make the ultimate sacrifice. But this sacrifice is not without reward. A few chapters earlier, Jesus had commented, "Very truly, I tell you, unless a grain of wheat falls into the earth and dies, it remains just a single grain; but if it dies, it bears much fruit" (12:24). Like the grain of wheat that dies, the love of which Jesus speaks bears much fruit. "I chose you . . . to go and bear fruit, fruit that will last" (15:16).

Mutuality now exists between Jesus and his disciples. They are no longer servants, but friends. And whatever they ask in Jesus' name will be granted to them by God—as if Jesus himself were asking.

Read together, the stories of Abraham and Moses as God's friends and Jesus' command to his disciples demonstrate that friendship with the divine

- is personal and intimate,
- is trusting and confident,

- evidences a willingness to sacrifice,
- participates in the mission,
- and is mutually beneficial.

Conclusion

But this is God we're talking about! We're not Abraham, Moses, or Jesus. Our definition of friendship includes doing good for the friend, mutuality, and betterment. How does that happen for God? How does one do good to or for God? The answer came to Etty Hillesum, the young Jewish woman whose diary, *An Interrupted Life*, described her internment at the Nazi concentration camp Auschwitz where she was eventually killed.

> But one thing is becoming increasingly clear to me: that You cannot help us, that we must help You to help ourselves. And that is all we can manage these days and also all that really matters: that we safeguard that little piece of You, God, in ourselves. And perhaps in others as well. Alas, there doesn't seem to be much You Yourself can do about our circumstances, about our lives. Neither do I hold You responsible. You cannot help us but we must help You and defend Your dwelling place inside us to the last.[33]

We do good for God whenever we seek to do God's will, watch out for God's interests. All friendship has—at its base—a common goal or interest shared by the friends. It's what brings people together and makes them friends. Basketball buddies love to play ball together. Bridge players are card friends. Likewise, friendship with God presumes we share with God the same desire, the same vision for the world and for all of creation. In our tradition that shared vision is the reign (or kingdom) of God. And as with our other friendships, seeking the good of the other actually makes us good as well. There is a mutuality of relationship in true friendship. And along the way we become better human beings because of our friendship with God.

For Reflection

- How would you describe your relationship with God? What experiences have led you to this understanding?

- What benefits might you see from becoming a friend of God? Is there a downside?

Colossians 1:24

Afterword

In the introduction, you were invited to make a friendship timeline and place on your timeline the friends you have made throughout your life. Return to that timeline and see if you have included your children, your spouse, and friends with whom you have had a falling out. Do you have work friends, comrades-in-arms, or other companions on your journey? Would you agree that your friends are those who have done good for you and shared mutuality in the relationship, and that you both are better people for the relationship?

Thomas Aquinas would argue that there is one friendship above all others for which we should strive.

> Thomas believes the unimaginable; in fact, he insists on it. Thomas believes we can, are called to be, and must be friends of God. That is what our life is, a life of ever-deepening friendship with a God who is our happiness, a colloquy of love given and love received, a sharing in which each friend delights in the goodness of the other, seeks their good, desires their happiness, and finally becomes one with them.[34]

We have attempted to investigate this claim by looking at our Scriptures. If we are to be friends of God then our Scriptures should give us direction. As Abraham,

Moses, and Jesus have shown us, we can be friends of God, delighting in the relationship and mutually working toward the reign of God. But our own personal friendships can also lead us to God. In our families, we learn the importance of honor, care, support, and encouragement. In marriage, presence, attraction, desire, and passion form the foundation of a relationship of mutual self-giving. These primary familial relationships provide the foundation for all future friendships. As we move beyond the home, we become open to other relationships. Our work colleagues or fellow students or neighbors become our companions on the journey, those who walk the way of life with us, sometimes giving us a hand to steady our steps and sometimes stepping on our toes. We may even encounter strangers whom at first glance we wouldn't think of as "friends," but who may indeed show us the deeper truths about ourselves as lovable and good.

The give and take of friendship matures us, increases our patience, and demands that we seek the good of the friend, even when they are imperfect, when they deny us or betray us. Finally, we must befriend ourselves if we hope to be a friend to others and to experience God's friendship. We have to accept our limitations, ask for forgiveness if that is needed, and trust that "God doesn't make junk," as the old bumper sticker says. We are made a little less than angels, and we need to learn to delight in our status as beloved children of God.

From family to companion to stranger to betrayer to self, our experiences of friendship prepare us for the ultimate relationship, which is friendship with God. All along the way, our experiences of friendship—*philia*—are leading us to love—*agapē*.

And so we conclude with a passage from the Book of Wisdom:

> Although [Wisdom] is but one, she can do all things, / and while remaining in herself, she renews all things; / in every generation she passes into holy souls / and makes them friends of God, and prophets; / for God loves nothing so much as the person who lives with wisdom. (Wisdom 7:27-28)

We have been pondering what friendship with God looks like and how one can be friends with God. And here is our answer.

We can't. At least not on our own initiative. Through God's Spirit, we are invited into that intimate relationship as friend. Wisdom passes into holy souls and thus friends of God are made. But while God initiates through the Spirit, it is left up to us to respond. As the passage suggests, we are to do two things. We are to dwell in Wisdom, here understood as dwelling in the spirit of God.

And we are to become prophets. It is not enough to be invited to be a friend of God. One must respond to that friendship. Abraham had to leave his home and family. Moses had to lead the people of God to the Promised Land. The disciples of Jesus had to demonstrate their friendship by loving one another, even to the point of giving up their lives for the sake of the Gospel. And what about us?

If we truly respond to God's invitation to be friends of God, are we also willing to be God's prophets?

Notes

1. *Analects* Book 1.1.

2. H. Rackham, trans., *Aristotle Nicomachean Ethics*, Loeb Classical Library (Cambridge, MA: Harvard University Press, 2003), 450.

3. Kisari Mohan Ganguli, trans., *The Mahabharata of Krishna-Dwaipayana Vyasa*, vol. 7 (Calcutta: Bharata Press, 1891), 370.

4. A. J. Arberry, *The Koran Interpreted: A Translation* (New York: Simon & Schuster, 1955), 215.

5. D. J. Enright and David Rawlinson, *The Oxford Book of Friendship* (Oxford: Oxford University Press, 1991), 96.

6. Vera Brittain, *Testament of Friendship: The Story of Winifred Holtby* (New York: MacMillan, 1940), 4.

7. A. C. Grayling, *Friendship* (New Haven: Yale University Press, 2013), 12.

8. Michel de Montaigne, *Essays*, trans. J. M. Cohen (Harmondsworth, Middlesex: Penguin Books, 1958), 95.

9. Harper Lee, *To Kill a Mockingbird* (Philadelphia: Lippincott, 1960), 84-85.

10. A. C. Grayling, *Friendship* (New Haven: Yale University Press, 2013), 53.

11. "friend, n. and adj." OED Online. Oxford University Press (accessed Jan. 2, 2019).

12. R. H. Hicks, *Diogenes Laertius, Lives of the Eminent Philosophers*, Loeb Classical Library (Cambridge, MA: Harvard University Press, 1925), 468.

13. William Armistead Falconer, *M. Tullius Cicero, De Amicitia*, Loeb Classical Library (Cambridge, MA: Harvard University Press, reprint 2007), 132.

14. Paul J. Wadell, *Friendship and the Moral Life* (Notre Dame, IN: University of Notre Dame Press, 1989), 128.

15. Aquinas, *Summa Theologica*, II-II, 24,2. Translation in Wadell, *Friendship and the Moral Life*, 123.

16. Wadell, *Friendship and the Moral Life*, 126-127.

17. Aelred of Rievaulx, *Spiritual Friendship*, ed. Marsha L. Dutton, trans. Lawrence C. Braceland (Collegeville, MN: Liturgical Press, 2010), 112-113.

18. Barbara E. Bowe, *Biblical Foundations of Spirituality: Touching a Finger to the Flame*, 2nd ed. (Lanham, MD: Rowman & Littlefield, 2017), 108-110.

19. Personal correspondence.

20. G. Walter Hansen, *The Letter to the Philippians* (Grand Rapids: Eerdmans, 2009), 11.

21. Saul M. Olyan, *Friendship in the Hebrew Bible* (New Haven: Yale University Press, 2017), 36.

22. Beryl Rawson, ed., *The Family in Ancient Rome: New Perspectives* (Ithaca, NY: Cornell University Press, 1986).

23. Paul J. Wadell, *The Primacy of Love: An Introduction to the Ethics of Thomas Aquinas* (New York: Paulist Press, 1992), 87.

24. Wadell, *Friendship and the Moral Life*, 121.

25. Samuel Laeuchli, "Origen's Interpretation of Judas Iscariot," *Church History* 22 (1953): 253-68.

26. Rodolphe Kasser, et al, trans. *The Gospel of Judas. Critical Edition: Together with the Letter of Peter to Phillip, James, and a Book of Allogenes from Codex Tchacos.* (Washington D.C.: National Geographic Society, 2007).

27. Ruth Etchells, *A Rainbow-coloured Cross: Personal Prayers with Easter Supplement* (London: SPCK, 2007), 168-169.

28. Eric Price, "Daniel Egan, 84, Drug Fighter Known as 'Junkie Priest,' Dies," New York Times (Feb. 13, 2000; accessed Dec. 29, 2018).

29. Wadell, *Primacy of Love*, 73.